Making
Boards Effective

Alvin Zander

Making Boards Effective

---

*The Dynamics of
Nonprofit Governing Boards*

Jossey-Bass Publishers · San Francisco

Substantial discounts on bulk quantities of Jossey-Bass books are available to corporations, professional associations, and other organizations. For details and discount information, contact the special sales department at Jossey-Bass Inc., Publishers. (415) 433-1740; Fax (415) 433-0499.

For sales outside the United States, contact Maxwell Macmillan International Publishing Group, 866 Third Avenue, New York, New York 10022.

Manufactured in the United States of America

 The paper used in this book is acid-free and meets the State of California requirements for recycled paper (50 percent recycled waste, including 10 percent postconsumer waste), which are the strictest guidelines for recycled paper currently in use in the United States.

10% POST CONSUMER WASTE

The ink in this book is either soy- or vegetable-based and during the printing process emits fewer than half the volatile organic compounds (VOCs) emitted by petroleum-based ink.

Library of Congress Cataloging-in-Publication Data

Zander, Alvin Frederick, date.
 Making boards effective : the dynamics of nonprofit governing boards / Alvin Zander. — 1st ed.
  p. cm. — (The Jossey-Bass nonprofit sector series)
(The Jossey-Bass management series)
 Includes bibliographical references (p.   ) and index.
 ISBN 1-55542-580-1 (acid-free paper)
 1. Nonprofit organizations—Management. 2. Directors of corporations. 3. Corporate governance. I. Title. II. Series. III. Series: The Jossey-Bass nonprofit sector series.
HD62.6.Z36 1993
658'.048—dc20   93-19577
                   CIP

FIRST EDITION
HB Printing 10 9 8 7 6 5 4 3 2 1   *Code 9379*

A joint publication in

The Jossey-Bass
Nonprofit Sector Series

and

The Jossey-Bass
Management Series

Contents

**Part Two: How Boards Work
Effectively with Constituents**

Preface

Almost every nonprofit organization has a governing board—a group with the right to provide rules, policies, and advice for the organization's personnel and the individuals they serve. A majority of these organizations could not exist without the support, enthusiasm, and work that board members provide. And many communities would be poorer places to live without the programs of nonprofit organizations that enhance their culture and welfare. Given the value of boards, it is useful for their members to understand how and why boards are effective. Why do board members behave as they do in performing their duties? How do these actions affect the board's performance? How can board members improve their board's way of working? Its productivity?

A common complaint about governing board members is that they fail to do the things they should and instead have the staff of the organization they monitor perform many of their duties. Why do they do this? Are items on the agenda uninteresting to them? Do they know too little to discuss issues with confidence? Does their chief officer solve problems with little effort and need only the board's approval, not its advice? Do nonmembers vigorously oppose members' views so that they tend to shy away from action? Do members feel uncomfortable with one another? Does the board's success mean little to them? Do they use poor procedures in making decisions? This book suggests ways to answer such questions and explains why many boards, in contrast, are lively, alert, and diligent.

My interest in the internal processes of boards and their relations with outsiders arose while I was writing a book about the ways in which activists pressure decision makers to change their beliefs and plans. In that book, *Effective Social Action by Community Groups* (Zander, 1990), I discussed how local advocacy units get started, choose their objectives, and try to influence official bodies (often governing boards) whose help they need. The current work is the obverse of that one. It considers how a formal body influences constituents effectively; responds to pressures such as demands, criticisms, or legal constraints arising outside the group; and resolves disagreements with external agents.

Purpose of This Book

The purpose of *Making Boards Effective* is to explain the nature of forces within governing boards and how board members deal with pressures originating from without. I explore actions members take to improve internal qualities of their boards, such as strength of mission, openness of discussion, effectiveness in making decisions, cooperative leadership, strong standards for group actions, and effective methods for settling disagreements among members. I discuss how members make their decisions acceptable to those who must live with the decisions, why members use one method rather than another in doing so, the constraints and pressures acting on boards, the origins of conflicts between boards and rival groups, and how boards settle disagreements with others. I offer practical suggestions for evaluating the performance of boards and improving their procedures. I do not treat leadership of a board as a separate topic, because the book is addressed to all responsible board members, including designated officials.

Few scholars who write about boards try to explain why certain conditions have specific effects—that is, what leads to what within a board. Most describe the duties of boards and the things they might do better. Their suggestions are based on their experience as board members, on their observations of boards, or on board practices described in published writings. However, many board inadequacies cannot be relieved by simply imitating the solutions of others. Dysfunctional aspects of a board can be treated more effectively by identifying and then modifying the causes. This book suggests ways to determine the cause and effect of phenomena within boards. The audience for this book includes those who serve on boards, are affected by board decisions, advise boards on how to improve their operation, and study the social psychology of boards.

My ideas for this book draw upon many sources: descriptions of boards in the popular media and in scholarly writings, reviews of research on the dynamics of groups, research on the motives and missions of groups and members, investigations of social power, studies of effective groups, work on making sound decisions, and investigations into social conflict and intergroup relations, as well as my own experiences on boards.

Overview of Contents

The book is divided into two parts. Chapters in the first section examine internal properties and processes of boards. Those in the second explain ways for boards to maintain good relations with constituents.

The Introduction describes the qualities of a strong board and how these are fostered by responsible members. Chapter One considers the motives of members, ways these motives are satisfied by board membership, and the importance of a clear and attainable mission for a board. Chapter Two examines the processes board members follow in making sound decisions. Chapter Three presents a number of attributes or processes that are fostered in boards to help make them effective. These include helping members to participate in discussions, sharing leadership within a board, choosing wise procedures for meetings, developing and maintaining strong group standards, benefiting from disputes among members, and selecting appropriate members.

In the second part of this work, Chapter Four describes how members of a board make their instructions acceptable to those affected by these directives. Chapter Five examines the kinds of constraints and pressures that boards face and how members respond to these factors. The ways in which a board increases its power to influence others are noted in Chapter Six. The causes of conflicts with external bodies are discussed in Chapter Seven. Chapter Eight considers a variety of ways in which a board can resolve a conflict with a protesting group. And, finally, Chapter Nine describes devices and methods members use in evaluating the performance of their board and improving its operation.

Walnut Creek, California　　　　　　　　　　　ALVIN ZANDER
July 1993

The Author

Alvin Zander has been a student of group behavior for many years. From 1948 to 1980, he was a program director in the Research Center for Group Dynamics at the University of Michigan. For twenty of those years he served as director of that center. As professor of psychology and of educational psychology, he has taught courses in the social psychology of groups. During his last seven years at Michigan, he served as the associate vice president for research. Zander is now retired from academic duties.

Zander earned his bachelor's degree (1936) in general science, his master's degree (1937) in public health, and his doctoral degree (1942) in psychology—all at the University of Michigan. He developed an interest in group behavior while employed as a graduate student during the Great Depression, helping small towns develop social services that they could not afford to obtain from professionals. After a postdoctoral year with Kurt Lewin at the University of Iowa (1942) and nearly three years as a clinical psychologist and a commissioned officer in the U.S. Public Health Service during World War II, Zander returned to the University of Michigan.

Zander has done research on the relations among people who differ in their ability to influence others, the impact of group membership on a person's self-regard, the nature of identification between people, the sources of members' motivation to help their group succeed, and the origins of a group's goals. He is coauthor of *Group Dynamics Research and Theory* (1968). He is author of *Motives and Goals in Groups* (1971), a presentation of results of a program of investigations; *Groups at Work* (1977), a discussion of needed research in group dynamics; *Making Groups Effective* (1982), a guide to fostering the development of well-functioning groups; *The Purposes of Groups and Organizations* (1985), an essay on the origins and objectives of social entities; and *Effective Social Action by Community Groups* (1990), an examination of how citizens generate changes in their towns through group effort.

Making
Boards Effective

Introduction
The Qualities of
an Effective Board

A group is a set of individuals who interact with and depend on each other. When members of a governing board discuss things, work together on regular duties, and count on colleagues to perform their part faithfully, their board fits this definition—it is a group. A board may be more like an audience and less like a group if its members sit quietly to hear officers' reports, ask questions infrequently, and seldom address one another. Such a board is a weak group. It derives little benefit from the ideas and talents of its members or from the give-and-take through which members create shared views.

A strong board is a better one for the organization it guides than is a weak board. A strong board has four main qualities. The first two, as already noted, identify it as a group: members interact freely and depend on the actions of each other. The second two help strengthen the group: members want to remain in the group and the board has the power to influence the people it is supposed to monitor. Responsible board members make a board strong by strengthening these four attributes within their unit and increasing their impact.

Members Interact Freely

In many groups, but especially in governing boards, members engage in a to-and-fro exchange of ideas to accomplish their goals.

1

Each interaction is necessary for members to define and understand their board's mission, set goals, make decisions, plan the implementation of decisions, support board officials, foster harmony in the board, influence targeted individuals, respond to external pressures on the group, settle conflicts with other groups, evaluate the board's performance, and devise better procedures for ensuring good performance.

Board members can create conditions in their group that encourage interaction among those members at a meeting. It is more likely that each member at a meeting will talk if the board is small. By small, I mean a group not larger than twenty members. A group of seven or eight members is optimal. In a small board, each member is likely to have more responsibilities than in a large board. Having several responsibilities heightens a person's interest in the work of his or her group (Barker and Gump, 1964; Cartwright and Zander, 1968). Small boards are less inhibiting to those at the table because members can get to know each other and feel more comfortable with one another. In a small board, members can use meeting time trying to understand what others are saying. In such a board, it is also possible to increase the amount of speech between particular members (where that is useful) by placing them across the table from each other; people address those individuals in front of them more than those next to them or at ends of the table (Steinzor, 1950).

A simple way to increase interaction between board members is to leave time on the agenda for discussion and to call for and welcome discussion. Interaction is further enhanced by giving members a chance to gather ideas through placing members in subgroups where the main issue is discussed, assigning several individuals to ask questions, showing films, engaging in role-playing, or scheduling brief presentations in which questions are posed for the board to consider. I discuss such methods further in Chapter Three.

Responsible members of a board can foster interaction through a statement to colleagues like the following: "We value speaking freely on this board. We want to be sure that everyone understands the information they receive and are satisfied with decisions we reach. The best way to achieve such aims is to talk, listen to others, and respond to their ideas."

Introduction

A presiding officer initiates discussion among men
or she welcomes comments that help the board move t
goals. The head of a board who sidetracks leadership actions by
members because he or she resents their acting as leaders dampens
discussion. A chairperson who urges participants to take a share in
the duties of leadership ensures lively participation; members feel
free to test other members' ideas against their own.

Members Depend on Each Other

For members to feel that they can count on one another's actions,
they need to understand what each member is saying in board meetings and why he or she makes those comments. Such understanding
is fostered through a cooperative relationship among members.

Members cooperate most when many of their goals are alike
and few are contradictory. For example, many trustees may have
personal goals of becoming better speakers, learning the history of
the organization monitored by the board, and developing the confidence a useful member needs to have. They may have goals for the
board such as running a successful financial campaign, setting clear
policies for the chief executive officer, and revising the board's
bylaws.

When members are in a cooperative relationship, they trust
each other's actions because they understand what each member is
trying to accomplish. They recognize that the moves of one member
help everyone, since all the members' goals are alike. Group
members welcome actions of colleagues that are for the good of each
and the group as a whole. Each member depends on what others
intend to accomplish and do accomplish.

Groups differ in their degree of cooperativeness. If group
members are very cooperative, they try to develop good procedures
for the board's work because the goals of each person and of the
group are more likely to be achieved through such procedures. They
press each other to do well because each has a vested interest in what
others provide. The members are friendly because they understand
and welcome each other's actions. They provide accurate information and expect such information from other members. The
members are pleased by the contributions of others (rather than

being envious) because they are not rivals. They welcome success by the group because this leads to more cooperation, which enhances the likelihood of further successes. They try to understand roles assigned to other members so they can collaborate smoothly. These qualities develop in a board simply because members depend on and trust one another.

Members Want to Remain in the Group

If a board provides a reasonable amount of satisfaction for its members, the members will be attracted to the group and want to stay in it. If membership is not satisfying, they will leave. The more members wish to remain in the board, the greater the cohesiveness of the board. Cohesiveness is greater among members when goals they hope to achieve on a board are more important and if they believe the chances of fulfilling their goals are good. If, for example, a member joins a board to make friends, advance the work of the organization the board oversees, or gain prestige from being part of an important group in the community, the member will be more attracted to the board when these desires are more important to that person, better fulfilled in the board than elsewhere, and likely to be satisfied in the future.

Members develop new sources of satisfaction as their experiences within a board teach them to have such desires. They may learn for the first time, for example, to like approval or acceptance by others, unselfish work, success as a member, protection from external agents (which the board provides), collaboration with others, or social power. They may stay on the board to have these experiences.

A person who accepts membership on a board has to forgo taking part in other groups. He or she must decide which group is more attractive, the board at hand or another group, and which group is a better place to spend the time and effort required of group membership. A person will join a board if membership in it is more attractive than comparable opportunities and will resign if competing memberships become more appealing. A person is more likely to join a board, moreover, and prize that membership if the values of other members are similar to those of the recruit (Scott, 1965).

As a result of belonging, members come to be more alike in their values and aspirations—they share the same hopes and feelings about what is right or wrong in their group's plans, programs, and procedures. Members conform more closely to rules and plans of their board as the entity grows in cohesiveness (Cartwright and Zander, 1968). In a board with high cohesiveness, members also work with and for each other in ways that help the group, more than in a board with low cohesiveness. In a cohesive board, members talk more, listen to others more closely, are more influenced by their colleagues, have greater impact on each other, attend board meetings more regularly, and more faithfully complete tasks for the board.

Board Has Power to Influence Nonmembers

Members of a governing board, more than members in most groups, make decisions about plans and policies they expect nonmembers to honor. Those people they wish to influence include the head officer and staff of the organization the board monitors, individuals who benefit from the services of the organization, and citizens who have an interest in the work of the organization and wish it well.

A basic requirement in ensuring that nonmembers accept a board's proposal is that it be based on a sound decision and valued by board members and those nonmembers who are to function in accord with it. A board can achieve good decisions more often, as will be seen in Chapter Two, if the procedures a board uses in making decisions are good. A decision is more acceptable to nonmembers, moreover, if it is true to the mission of the board because such a decision moves all concerned toward ends the board hopes to achieve.

Board members may strongly support a decision they have made but will not be able to persuade others to abide by it unless they initiate the change without generating resistance among those to whom the decision is addressed. By *resistance*, I mean an emotional response (anger, fear, dismay) among receivers of the board's message that is aroused in them by the style the board uses in delivering instructions, not by the content of the proposal. *Opposition*, in contrast, refers to disagreement with the substantive meaning of a message (see Chapters Six and Seven). Board members make an action more acceptable to nonmembers by arousing a given desire in listeners (for example, a desire for achievement, acceptance in the community, or better service to clients of the agency) and by helping the nonmembers recognize that the change being proposed will satisfy that desire (see Chapter Four).

A board is more likely to win a favorable response among those it wishes to influence if it is a legitimate entity, that is, one that the nonmembers know has the right to make requests, even demands, which they have the duty to obey. A board wins legitimacy in several ways: legislation by a state, community, or large association that requires that the board be established; the board's support of values that are important to those who accept its mandates: or election of members of the board by those who are to abide by the board's decisions. The actions of a legitimate board are regularly respected and accepted by persons under the power of that board.

If a board does not win acceptance of a proposal after announcing it, the board may turn to procedures that allow little choice for persons who are to abide by the directive. It is likely that few nonprofit boards use coercion to obtain obedience from constituents; they prefer to use ways that help targeted groups become enthusiastic about a change, as discussed in Chapter Four. Boards that press, urge, reward, or coerce in order to get their way need to know what they are doing and why (see Chapter Six).

A board can be more effective in relations with others if members know how to prevent conflicts with opposing groups and how to resolve conflicts should they arise. A conflict exists when two parties disagree about what they should or should not do. Conflict is more likely to develop under particular conditions and worsen under others, as described in Chapter Seven. A board needs to have plans for settling disagreements with other groups (see Chapter Eight).

Summary

A governing board is a strong group if responsible members strengthen four attributes of their unit and increase the impact of each within that body:

1. Members interact freely because they are encouraged to do so and conditions are created within the board that make a to-and-fro exchange of ideas easy.
2. Members depend on each other because they have similar goals for themselves and their group and because they understand one another's aims and roles.
3. Members want to remain in the group because they derive satisfaction from participating in the unit.
4. Their board has power to influence the behavior and beliefs of nonmembers whose actions the board is expected to monitor and guide.

Part One

---

*What Goes On Inside
the Effective Board*

1

Common Purpose
Aligning Mission, Goals, and Motives

In an effective board, members know what they want to accomplish personally, believe their board's purpose is important, choose an efficient path for attaining objectives, want to improve their board's productivity, and try to avoid time-wasting distractions. In an ineffective board, in contrast, members appear bored at meetings and have little to say and their meetings get nowhere. Members of an effective board work, in general, to fulfill self-oriented motives, group-oriented motives, or both.

Self-Oriented Motives

People who become members of a governing board bring personal motives with them to the board. They want, for example, to find friends, develop skills, pick up specific information, win approval, attain prestige, or engage in activities the board sponsors. A recruiter for a board tries to discover what kinds of goals are important to a potential member and tells that person which goals he or she will be able to fulfill on the board and those the individual cannot hope to meet. Some board officers enhance a newcomer's satisfaction by helping him or her have experiences, successes, learnings, or opportunities that satisfy that individual's needs.

A member, as noted earlier, develops new desires while on a board. Satisfying these desires often becomes more attractive to the member than meeting goals he or she originally brought to the group. Examples of acquired goals include a desire to be an influential member, an officer of the board, a winner over rival colleagues, a provider of special knowledge, or a solver of problems the board must answer.

Often, a board is urged by external critics to set specific objectives. These critics may be citizens in the community, leaders of the staff monitored by the board, or representatives of interested organizations. Usually, these people seek actions that will benefit them, such as the development of a new program, the allotment of more funds to meet their needs, the devaluing of the demands of others, or the banning of certain books from the library (Zander, 1990). On other occasions, nonmembers help board members take pride in their work, hoping this will encourage them to continue good efforts. Nonmembers may say to board members, "You can be proud of the contribution you are making," "Keep up the good work in our behalf," "You clearly like and admire one another— a good thing," or "People in town look up to this board." Such approving comments can create the desire for more praise in board members.

Board members' self-oriented motives affect their actions and beliefs. A person who joins a board with an eye toward finding new friends, for example, will emphasize socializing, interacting with likable associates, agreeing with colleagues, fostering harmony, or suppressing disagreements. Someone who thinks a board may be a means to win prestige will try to get a place on a high-status board, run for an office in the board, use the board as a means to become well known, or work hard on a public task so that his or her work is noticed. Someone who seeks membership in order to reform a board's goals or actions will look for allies who think as he or she does, find fault with current leaders, disapprove of aims and methods of the board, or encourage like-minded nonmembers to come before the board and voice their complaints.

Group-Oriented Motives

Sometimes, all members of a board have exactly the same motive, and the strength of the board is enhanced because members work together toward that aim. They decide together how to achieve the desired end state, for example, salvation for sinners, accreditation for their school system, greater beauty in the community, a successful campaign for their candidate, or more power for their union's local. In my examination of the purposes of three hundred associations of all sizes (Zander, 1971, 1972), I found that two-thirds of these groups existed to help their members work toward a common self-oriented purpose. Each association was in effect a large self-help group. One-third intended to help society or people who were not members of the association (Zander, 1971, 1972).

Intuitively, most members of a board recognize and research (Locke and Latham, 1990; Larson and LaFasto, 1989) also shows that groups with a stated goal do better than ones that try to do their best in the same activity with no goal in mind. Thus, members prefer to set a goal for a job their board has to do repeatedly.

An interesting sequence of steps occurs as board members think about what their board ought to accomplish and how its members should behave. First, a member privately considers what goals he or she wants to achieve for his or her own good while on the board. Second, the member's decision on that issue affects the goal he or she thinks the board should have for the task it is planning to take in hand; the member wants the group to work toward ends that will benefit him or her to some degree. Third, the goal the member prefers the board to have, along with ones other members propose, determines the shared goal, that is, the board's goal for the board. Fourth, this joint agreement affects what kind of goal the group will create for each member and what each member should therefore achieve for the good of the group—the board's goal for the member. Fifth, the member, in light of the above information, decides what personal goal he or she now wants, and the above cycle starts again and continues. Thus, a circular causal system develops between members' personal goals and a board's selection of its goals. Board members achieve satisfaction when a goal for the self, the group, or both is reached (Zander, 1971).

Members usually decide as a group on goals for their board. If the goals they choose are in accord with their own aims, they readily cooperate in working toward those objectives. Each member sees that his or her chances of satisfying personal needs are increased as other members work toward the board's goal. Thus, the interaction of the group is supportive and friendly. Members trust one another; know they can say what they wish when communicating with each other; listen to what other members have to say; and feel free to be persuasive, where that is necessary.

If, in contrast, members cannot agree on a common goal and rivalry arises among members because their aims differ, the atmosphere of a board meeting is different. Each member feels at a disadvantage when other members say useful things. Each is suspicious of the other members' intentions and seldom talks or talks in misleading ways. Members are in a competitive relationship and each tries to perform better than any other member (Deutsch, 1973).

Some objectives that members may want their board to attain include greater influence in the community, harmony among participants, increased membership, or achievement of goals that are true to the board's mission. The achievement of objectives may be measured by the amount of money to be collected during an annual fundraising campaign, space to be found for new programs, number of volumes to be added to the library, amount of racial and ethnic diversity to be developed on the board, or an agreement to collaborate with the board of another organization nearby. When a board achieves such a goal, members have pride in their group, unless attaining the goal was so easy that it provided little challenge.

Members who have a strong desire for their board to succeed, compared to ones who have little such desire, do things more often that help their board succeed (Zander, 1971, 1982). They make comments that reveal their eagerness to have colleagues work hard on a task. They encourage and praise other colleagues and ways of improving the board's procedures. They indicate that they are prepared to do things the board must accomplish by showing interest in the activity, saying they want to do well, expecting others to exert effort, wanting to do better than similar boards have done on this task, and anticipating that members will help one another. They assist the board by working hard, developing the skills they need to achieve a goal, reducing their rate of errors, helping associates, and considering how to improve the quality of the board's work. They seek precise information about the quality of their board's product and that of rival groups to be sure their board does better than other boards. These members set personal goals in accord with the board's goals and are prouder of their board's output than of their individual contributions to the group's activity. They are, in short, actively involved in helping their board achieve goals that are important to the group. Their behavior and beliefs attest to their desire for the board's success.

Members of a board develop a keener desire for its success when they learn how their board performed on a task for which they initially had no firm goal. If they repeat an activity and learn their board's score after each trial, board members become able to judge how well their board might do on the task the next time. The board thus develops an informal goal, a rough criterion of excellence, and an indicator of how well the board must perform to satisfy its members.

When a board reaches a goal or does better than the goal, members are proud of their board. This feeling of pride stimulates interest in further success. Typically, board members want to do better the next time, so they set a harder goal. Their satisfaction is increased if they attain increasingly difficult goals. Members of most boards feel pressure from several sources to raise their sights and set higher goals for a task every time they attempt to achieve it.

A board leader encourages board members to have pride in their achievements by doing such things as the following:

1. Emphasizing the sources of pride in the board, what causes pride to develop among members, and what consequences pride has for the board. Veteran members often pass along such ideas to newcomers.
2. Increasing the members' desire for their board to be successful by arranging the board's goals, procedures, work plans, and resources to help the board achieve its goals. An excellent outcome to a project does not dull members' taste for further success, as is often said. Instead, it makes high-quality work more desirable to members.
3. Helping the board set clear goals. Members cannot feel successful if they are uncertain about whether they have attained

the board's objective or what they must do to attain the objective.

4. Selecting goals that are realistic challenges for members, not unreasonably hard or easy ones. The board's goals are standards of excellence for members; therefore, the goals must not be conducive to failure.

5. Making sure each member understands what his or her contribution is and that this contribution is valued.

6. Indicating to members how belonging to the board has been helpful to them as individuals so that each member views the board as an attractive group and wants to remain in it.

7. Making it clear to all members that each member depends on the work of the others if the board is to complete its task.

8. Changing goals that turn out to be too difficult to achieve. Group pride comes from living up to reasonable expectations, not from failing impossibly difficult goals.

9. Considering what obstacles might prevent fulfillment of selected goals and how the board can overcome these obstacles.

10. Encouraging frank talk in meetings about how the process and performance of the board can be improved and boring parts of the task can be made more interesting.

11. Avoiding fear of failure and the way it causes the group to avoid challenges rather than accept them.

12. Helping members feel responsible for their group's fate so that each knows that the group depends on his or her efforts and wants to improve the quality of his or her contribution. Telling a member that he or she is needed, useful, and eligible for equal shares of any approval or reward won by the board can help to make that person feel responsible for the fate of the group.

13. Giving members assignments that suit their abilities and make it possible for them to feel competent. Capable members develop a stronger desire for board success because they perform well on their group's task. Those members who think they are not competent because they are given duties that are too hard for them become concerned about their personal failures and lose interest in the group's goals.

The members' desire to see that the organization guided by their board is successful is another kind of motivation, similar to the foregoing in its operation and effects. This type of motivation is, more precisely, the capacity of trustees to be satisfied when the nonprofit organization they monitor attains goals set for it by the board and to feel at fault if that organization fails. Because the board hires the chief executive officer of the organization and sets goals and policies that encourage or limit his or her action, the success or failure of the organization is due in large part to the actions of board members. Board members are more likely to want the organization to succeed when they provide help in the organization's programs through such activities as: taking tickets at a play, helping run a track meet, soliciting funds, singing in a choir, advising on interior decoration, transporting patients, or tutoring troubled children.

A member's desire to see the organization succeed can be as strong or stronger than a self-oriented motive or a wish for the board to succeed. Some members stay with an unattractive board because they want to make sure that the church, school, clinic, or library under their board's care prospers. Or a board member may be most motivated to improve conditions in the local community and most satisfied when the community benefits through the board's efforts.

A board member's desires to achieve goals set for the self, board, organization, or community are additive; that is, the greater the number of motives influencing a board member's behavior, the more eager the member is to achieve goals set for these separate entities. Leaders of a board need to keep in mind, however, that separate motives can work against each other (Forward, 1969). For example, a member who uses the board to gain publicity for his or her political future may protest intentions of colleagues that are not beneficial to the member and weaken board actions by doing so. Or a board member may so strongly want the board to succeed that he or she does things that harm rather than benefit the organization the board guides.

Broad and Specific Objectives

A board's goal can be described as a desirable state of affairs members intend to bring about through joint efforts. Because attainment of a goal requires collaboration among trustees, the goal is usually chosen by common agreement. An important aspect of such a group decision is that members publicly promise each other they will prize the chosen objective and work together toward its attainment. The goal is the board's standard of excellence.

Larson and LaFasto (1989, p. 27), in a study of the qualities that characterize successful and unsuccessful teams in government, business, and sports, note that "in every case, without exception, when an effectively functioning team was identified, it was described by the respondent as having a clear understanding of its objective. . . . The explanation for the team's ineffectiveness involved, in one sense or another, the goal." Team members forget or turn away from their goal, according to Larson and LaFasto, if they disagree on what the group's goal is or mainly try to satisfy self-centered schemes.

Mission Statement

Some goals are broad and abstract, others are narrow and precise. A board's grandest and highest purpose or mission, what the board wants to do and for whom, is described as an abstract objective in a statement of mission or purpose. Such a statement is value loaded because it elucidates the good things a board and organization intend to accomplish or the benefits they wish to generate for other people. The mission statement guides the selection of smaller and more exactly defined objectives.

Let us examine the mission statements of some organizations. The mission of the Athena Club in a midwestern town is to "improve the culture of the community." The mission of the Rotary Club "is to encourage and foster the ideal of service as a basis of worthy enterprise." The mission of the Community Club in Rossmoor, a village of elderly persons, is "to promote civic knowledge and appreciation of Rossmoor, and understanding of its plan of operation; and to promote and support measures affecting its continuing success as an outstanding attractive community." The mission statement of John F. Kennedy University says that the school "was founded with the belief that access to education is a lifelong right for all who earnestly seek it. The University is dedicated to mature students who want to continue their education, find new directions, and discover higher meaning for their lives. . . . Our rigorous academic programs foster intellectual inquiry and enable our graduates to master theoretical knowledge, gain a sense of personal power and acquire the skills to perform effectively in their chosen fields." Board members working toward laudable missions like these believe they are "doing good," even though they may have little objective evidence that they are attaining such broad goals.

A statement of a group's mission, as in the examples above, says nothing about how the mission will be fulfilled or what procedures among an endless variety of possibilities will be used in fulfilling it. The description of the mission merely helps board members to be sure that activities conducted by the board or the staff are in accord with the board's general purpose.

Vision

Some boards try to develop a vision of the organization in the future to foster thinking about how they can fulfill their mission. The vision may describe, for example, operating programs, participants, facilities, or finances in ten years. A vision suggests what eventual solutions of currently difficult problems may be.

A club that aims to improve culture in its community, for example, may have a statement of its vision that says, "We will have a program of five concerts . . . the dance classes will be overcrowded and eight plays on the schedule for the civic theater." The vision of John F. Kennedy University, developed by a committee of faculty and staff members, says that the school "will be known for its high educational standards, quality, innovation and creativity. The University will be a dynamic and rewarding place to study, teach, and work in an environment in which life-long relationships are developed. It will have a style of management which involves faculty, staff, and students in planning, problem-solving, and decision making. The University will be a financially secure institution with income from a variety of sources. It will secure a permanent campus in order to provide appropriate facilities to fulfill its mission." This school's vision statement, one can see, makes work toward the school's mission imaginable but says little about what means will be used to attain these results.

Goals

To be useful, a goal must, of course, be in accord with the mission the board has agreed upon. A board's goal, in contrast to its purpose or mission, is stated in concrete language. It names accomplishments to be achieved in a given period of time, such as the number of patients to be treated, animals to be rescued, dollars to be solicited, souls to be saved, books to be loaned, games to be won, or homeless to be housed.

A subgoal is a level of achievement that, if attained, helps toward the accomplishment of a larger objective. It is the goal the group or individual must reach on the way to a more important end. For example, a Boy Scout works to win a merit badge in Morse code (the subgoal) so that he can improve his chances of becoming an Eagle Scout (the larger objective). Members of the air force at a training school on emergency survival try to complete a four-day trek through deep snow (the subgoal) so they can become eligible for a promotion (the end goal) (Thomas and Zander, 1959).

The more members of a group prize a main goal, the more they value a subgoal on the way to the important end. An officer of a board increases members' interest in a dull activity by reminding them that this step must be completed before they can move to a larger and more satisfying task. For example, the names and histories of potential candidates must be assembled and the candidates must be interviewed before board members can turn to choosing a new chief executive officer.

Sometimes boards choose hollow goals. These unattractive activities are performed because the group's stated purposes are so ambiguous, unmeasurable, and unattainable that members cannot know whether or not they are reaching them. Trustees are not able to determine, for example, if their activities actually improve the local culture, help students discover higher meanings for their life, promote greater civic knowledge, or foster better understanding of the brotherhood of mankind. Thus, the board members cannot tell if they have succeeded or failed in such missions.

To be able to measure what they have accomplished, the board members often create goals whose attainment (or failure) can be accurately determined but that may have little relevance to their broader goals. For example, instead of worrying about salvation for churchgoers, members of the board of a church put their prime interest in, and judge their organization's success by, the amount of income in the collection plate each Sunday, the number of new members each year, or the approval of their congregation by officials of their denomination. Instead of attending to the effectiveness of teaching in the classroom or the quality of learning by students, a school board may develop more interest in the number of stories about the board in the local newspaper or the absence of complaints by parents at board meetings. Such simple goals lead board members to concentrate on aims that are concrete, easy to work on, and clear indicators of the board's performance, regardless of whether they suit the group's mission (Zander, 1985). Board members are less likely to set such meaningless goals if their unit's purpose is clear; that is, members know how to achieve it and can accurately tell when they have done so.

Each goal has characteristics that affect how well members live up to it and how much satisfaction they derive from attaining it. Examples of such characteristics and their effects are described in my previous work (Zander, 1985). The characteristics of goals include: importance (the size of change the accomplishment of a goal creates in a board, its members, or the organization supervised by the board), power (the degree of influence the goal has on the behavior of board members), flexibility (the ease with which the goal can be modified), and consonance (how well the goal fits with other goals of the board). Three additional characteristics of a goal will be discussed at more length here: accessibility, measurability, and difficulty.

The *accessibility* of a board's objective relates to whether members know methods they can use to move toward their goal. A goal's degree of accessibility is determined by the likelihood, as members see it, that potential actions will lead to achieving the goal. It also is determined by observing whether a board's programs, projects, procedures, or policies bring it closer to its goal. Once a method has led to the achievement of a goal, it presumably can do so another time. The goal has accessibility: means to achieve it are known and it can in fact be reached.

The notion of accessibility implies that not all activities by board members are relevant in reaching the board's larger goals. And a goal may be accessible but unmeasurable; that is, a procedure to attain a goal may be known, but how to measure its attainment is not known. For example, board members may be aware of how their organization can teach morality to children but may not be sure what criteria to use in judging its success. Such a condition— accessible but unmeasurable—will not last long. Evaluation of a potential path's value depends not only on understanding where board members want their organization to go but also on whether it has arrived.

The *measurability* of a group's goal indicates how reliably the actual achievement of that goal can be determined. A measurable objective indicates exactly what should change and by how much and what events or data are to be taken as evidence that the goal has been reached. If, for example, the trustees of a college want their school to be more widely known, how can they be sure they have achieved this goal? Shall they judge movement toward the goal by the number of requests for school catalogues, the number of news stories about the school in area newspapers, the speeches made about the college by board and staff members, the success of their school's basketball team, their gut feeling that the school is becoming notable, or the number of students transferring from other schools?

Clearly, the type of data board members need to determine if their board has achieved its objective differs for different goals. However, a precisely stated goal describes what things should change and in what ways so that misinterpretation about the actual attainment of the goal is precluded. Because nonprofit organizations intend to make a difference for those people they reach, it is not uncommon for the missions and objectives of such groups to be stated in unmeasurable terms. Nonprofit organizations tend to have high-minded missions stated in abstract terms; thus, their broad purposes are often unmeasurable.

The *difficulty* of a board's goal is determined by the amount of energy, ability, time, or resources required to achieve that goal.

When board members are deciding what goal their board ought to have, they of course recognize that there is less chance of achieving a hard goal than an easy one. Even so, a more difficult goal almost always has greater appeal because members believe they will get more satisfaction from achieving a higher aspiration than from attaining a lower one. Members believe that by choosing a harder goal they will get more done, receive more approval, and feel prouder of their group. They also sense that they will not be proud of reaching a goal their group has regularly achieved. And they will not be embarrassed if their group falls short of an objective that is more difficult than any the board has ever been able to reach, but they will be ashamed if they fall short on a task they have previously reached with ease. Thus, board members prefer to aim high. Anyone who has observed boards will tell you that most boards usually want to aim for unrealistically high ends.

Effect of a Board's Success or Failure on Members

Examining the reaction of board members to their success in meeting a goal or their failure to meet a goal provides valuable insight. For example, a board of a local United Fund campaign sets a goal each year in terms of dollars to be solicited, calculates its intake for that year, and sets a new objective for the next fundraising campaign in light of its performance in the current year plus information (provided by the national headquarters) about what other towns collected. In a study with colleagues (Zander, Forward, and Albert, 1969) I identified twenty-three United Community Fund boards that reached their campaign goal four years in a row and twenty-three that failed four years in a row. Within each board, information was obtained by questionnaire from the four most influential and actively involved board members (identified by the hired leader of the local staff) and the four who were least influential. Members of the boards of the groups that consistently failed, compared to members of successful groups, repeatedly set their goals too high (in light of their recent income); wanted to do away with setting annual goals; and gave lower ratings to their board as a whole, campaign solicitors, and the effectiveness of their chapter in serving the community.

The strong leaders of each board had a stronger desire that the board be successful than did the members on the fringe. Regardless of their fund's success, central members, in contrast to peripheral ones, were generally more confident that their group would do well in the future, saw more value in raising its goal, opposed lowering the goal, praised their chapter's performance, rated their personal contribution high, worked hard during campaigns, and planned to continue working hard in the future. If their fund was consistently successful, leaders derived satisfaction from their group's efforts and believed that future successes were assured. In a failing fund, the central board members felt worse than the peripheral ones and felt more obliged to set unreasonable difficult goals and more ready to work toward irrational aims, even if they had to do most of the work themselves.

All in all, influential board members, in contrast to peripheral ones, were more deeply interested in the process of setting goals and in the quality of their organization's performance. The central members on the United Fund boards displayed what has often been observed in research on groups; namely, more responsible members feel the success of their group or its failure more fervently than members who are not active participants (Medow and Zander, 1965; Zander and Newcomb, 1967; Zander, 1971).

As might be expected, board members tend to select a goal for their board that will provide as much satisfaction after a success or as little dissatisfaction after a failure as possible. The goal must be difficult enough to provide satisfaction when achieved but not so difficult that it cannot be met. In short, the goal would be a moderate challenge; that is, a bit, not too much, harder than the one most recently accomplished.

After a board succeeds, board members chose a more difficult goal for the future. If a board fails, members typically do not change the goal, or they lower it slightly. As a result, over time, a board's average goals are above the average level it attains. Thus, boards fail to attain their goals more often than they succeed.

External groups often pressure board members to select more difficult goals. For example, people who depend on the board, such as teachers, clients, staff members, or parents, want the board to provide more services, better pay, improved facilities, or changes in programs—all of which increase costs and are difficult to achieve. Comparable agencies in other towns may do better than the local one, and this news arouses demands for more from the local board. Editorial writers, members of a city council, alumni of a local college, or financial supporters of an organization may make unfavorable comments about a board's lack of ambition and urge it to aim higher. Or a board may receive a direct order from a superior who has the right to place demands on it. Other sources of external pressure are leaders in the local organization, officers of an association of which the local unit is a chapter, or officials in a central office of an organization with many branches. More often than not, a superior wants a better performance from the board or the organization it monitors.

A series of failures motivates members to avoid the embarrassment and other undesirable consequences of failure instead of working for success. A desire to avoid the effects of failure makes board members uncertain about what goal they should choose for their group: a very easy one that they can comfortably achieve or a very hard one that they might fail to achieve but that might earn them mild applause for a good try. The odds are great that members would rather work to reduce the chances of embarrassment than to succeed on a task that provides no satisfaction, because it is so easy; they sense there is a better likelihood, in light of their past record, of decreasing embarrassment than of increasing pride (Zander, 1971, 1977).

Board members who are more concerned about avoiding shame than about succeeding tend to do things that will protect them. They say that the goal was not a challenge because it was not hard enough, goal setting should be abolished, attaining the goal is not worth the effort, no one really cares if they attain their board's goal, they do not mind failing, other members did not try, or the board's procedures were not correct. A strong fear of failure causes board members to make excuses and to disparage the task they failed at.

Board members may also choose unrealistic goals because of lack of accurate evidence about how well their group is performing. They may be unable to get this information because the group's purpose is vague (unmeasurable) and they are not able to evaluate their group's performance. When feedback on their board's output is not available or is untrustworthy, members' hopes for success typically determine their reaction, and they tend to believe that the output of their group has been good (no news is good news) (Zander, 1971, 1977).

Choosing Realistic Goals

Because board members often choose unreasonably difficult goals, board leaders must reduce the impact of conditions that pressure members toward such choices and help members choose more sensible objectives. Given the unwelcome consequences of failing to achieve a board's goal, responsible board members usually want to prevent failure. Ideally, as was noted earlier, a group chooses a goal that is moderately challenging, neither too hard nor too easy. Therefore, the goal should be at a level just a bit higher than what the board has attained previously.

Having accurate information about the board's past performances ensures that goal setters do not have false ideas about the ability of the board. Another way to ensure that reasonable goals are set is to state a board's objective as precisely as possible so that it is a measurable criterion for evaluating the group's output. Or a board leader can help members to value the consequences of success by emphasizing the pride members will have in themselves and their board when it succeeds.

Board members who desire to succeed develop a preference for moderately challenging goals because they want a goal they can attain. Board leaders should play down the fear of what can happen if the board fails and reduce members' fear about being embarrassed if the board does poorly. Comparing the group's performance to the work done by comparable boards helps members set reasonable goals. Or members can be encouraged to introduce changes in the board's processes that enable them to work effectively for their board and the organization they guide.

It is useful to make sure that no member "is lost in the crowd," or feels his or her contribution is not noteworthy because others are already doing what needs to be done. Failing to participate in a group is called *social loafing*—a reduction in effort by some group members when many are jointly responsible for completing a task. An individual may, for example, make a conscious decision not to take part on the assumption that a good performance by him or her will not be approved of or will be resented by others in the group. The person may not participate because he or she views doing so as futile. Or the person may become anxious and thus perform below his or her usual skill level (Mullen and Baumeister, 1987). Generally speaking, a board's leader needs to give anyone he or she suspects of loafing an assignment that makes that person's actions both visible in and important to the board. Otherwise, these members will not develop much desire for success by their board or work toward that end.

Summary

Members' efforts while serving on a board are driven by several kinds of motives. They seek to satisfy personal hopes they bring with them or learn to value from experience as a board member. These motives affect the goals they want the board to set for itself. They develop a desire for their board to succeed and are satisfied when that body attains the goals members set for it. Members' desire for achievement by their board can be enhanced if board members aspire to have the organization they are guiding achieve objectives the board creates for it, or they want the community served by the organization to benefit from its activities. The strength of members' motives for themselves, the board, the organization, and the community is additive.

A board's goal is a desirable state of affairs members intend to bring about through joint efforts. Some goals are broad, abstract, and describe the board's grandest and highest purpose of mission: the good things a board and organization intend to accomplish. Other goals are narrow and precise, are stated in concrete language, and name accomplishments to be achieved in a given period of time. Some boards develop a vision of their unit or organization in the future in order to stimulate their thinking about how they can fulfill their goals.

Goals differ in characteristics that affect how well members live up to the goal and how much satisfaction they derive from attaining the goal. The accessibility of a board's objective indicates whether members know methods they can use to move toward the goal. The measurability of a group's goal relates to how reliably members can determine if their unit has achieved the goal. The difficult of a board's goal is determined by the amount of energy, ability, time, or resources required to achieve the goal.

Board members tend to prefer a difficult goal because they believe they will get more satisfaction from reaching one that is harder to achieve. As a result, boards fail more often than they succeed. A series of failures motivates members, instead of working for a success, to avoid the embarrassment and other consequences of failure by derogating the task, wishing to avoid setting a goal, saying that attainment of the goal is not worth the effort or that colleagues therefore did not try, and protecting themselves in other ways.

Members can be helped to choose realistic goals for their board by giving them accurate information about their (and comparable groups') performances, stating the goal in precise terms, enhancing their desire to achieve success, and preventing social loafing among the members.

2

Core Work

Solving Difficult Problems and Making Good Decisions

Although board members occasionally feel their meetings accomplish little, I suspect they more often sense their meetings are useful and that governance by a board is better than allowing an executive officer to function without the advice or approval of trustees. Many nonprofit organizations, especially universities, hospitals, churches, libraries, professional groups, and so on, are registered as corporations and are legally required to have boards. Why do members of a board value their role? Why do legislators require institutions to have governing boards?

An answer to both of these questions is that activities of nonprofit organizations have an impact on community life. The services of an organization are more likely to be acceptable to clients, citizens, patients, or parents if the organization's programs are monitored by a board made up of people who know the views of the community. A governing board can ensure that the staff of its organization provides services that benefit the community.

The decisions a board makes in guiding a nonprofit organization are usually matters of judgment. Typically, the board members' wisdom and experience play a large part in these decisions. For example, board members may need to answer questions like the following: Which candidate for the top staff position is best? Should we ban particular books from the library? Where can we get more funds? What kind of service can we provide for the

29

homeless? Should we modify our main mission? On questions like these, board members offer different opinions that are drawn from their special skills or interests, pool resources they bring with them, or ask for help from friends who can offer useful advice. They check and test each other's thinking during discussions and eventually come up with an answer, perhaps not the best answer but one that satisfies them to a reasonable degree.

Nonprofit boards seldom have to answer questions on their own that have only one correct solution, demand special expertise, or require logical thought, such as: How much can we save by eliminating the Department of Geography? Will the beams supporting our roof hold up for another winter? What is wrong with our furnace? Can we legally build a public structure on that land? Boards seek the advice of trained consultants on questions like these or give the question to informed board members who gather expert information and do the reasoning necessary for finding the right answer. When there is only one correct outcome, facts and logic are better than discussions among trustees.

Discussing problems and deciding on solutions increases board members' eagerness to develop sound plans. When a decision is adopted, moreover, those who had a part in making it are committed to it and want to make sure the decision is implemented. Boards become devoted to solutions they help devise. Boards will not benefit from their members offering separate views about problems, however, if members hold to their own positions and do not listen to the ideas of others or if they seek a solution, any solution, so they can end a meeting. How do boards decide important question most efficiently and usefully?

The Problem-Solving Process

The need for board members to work toward a decision arises while they are engaged in a broader activity called *problem solving*. The distinction between solving a problem and making a decision is not important in many situations because one seldom occurs without the other, but the two processes differ in the range of their activities. In the problem-solving process, members must attend closely to matters in several stages before and after a decision is made. Decision making is but a single step in the problem-solving process. To trace the development of the problem-solving process and put decision making in its proper setting, let us first define some terms.

A *problem* for a board is a specific situation to which members must respond if the group is to function effectively. The members face a *dilemma* if they have no immediately useful response to the problem. In a *group problem-solving process,* members identify alternative ways of dealing with the situation and then select the most satisfactory course, or the *solution.* A solution to a board's problem is therefore a response that alters the specific situation so that it no longer causes a dilemma. Thus, *board decision making* is the selection of one preferred solution from among several alternatives. If there is no problem, no decision is needed, and things continue as they are, unless a need for a decision arises because members wish to make an improvement in the board or organization they monitor.

The problem-solving process moves through several stages. Four of the primary stages are

1. Defining the problem that needs a response and deciding why a response is necessary
2. Identifying a number of potential solutions to the problem
3. Deciding on the best solution among these alternatives (making the decision)
4. Taking action to implement the decision

Each stage will be discussed in this chapter and then typical difficulties in making decisions and methods for improving the quality of deliberations will considered.

A problem is worthy of consideration by a board if its resolution can create a material change in the institution, involve the transfer of property, initiate a new enterprise, require a transformation in a long-standing procedure, cost more than the board may spend, or is known to have ardent pro-and-con advocates. On this kind of topic, board members must clarify why a change is necessary and state their proposals in precise language so a misunderstanding will not ensue.

Colleagues on a board feel a problem is crucial if they judge a current situation to be undesirable and in need of correction. They might not wish to improve matters, however, if doing so would be too difficult or costly. They may justify inaction by saying the situation is not too bad, is to be expected, or is a regular part of life in any organization. Board members take firm remedial steps, in contrast, if they believe that they and constituents are enduring more than they should or are receiving fewer benefits than they deserve, compared to what they ought to get or what others obtain. They are in a state of "relative deprivation."

There is no simple relationship between the severity of a given problem and the perception that it places people at a disadvantage. Before a majority of board members will feel they should deal with a questionable situation, they must be convinced that the situation is intolerable and that all members agree with that view. Members who support a need for a change point out that other organizations have advantages theirs does not, such as better facilities, smaller costs, larger laboratories, more trained staff members, more services, higher wages, or bigger budgets. Constituents are told as well that those with a better deal do not deserve it any more than they do. Hesitant board members may be stirred to act if they are shown that practices they approved do not conform to usual standards in matters such as disposing of toxic waste, meeting fire-safety codes, hiring minority members, or adhering to zoning regulations.

Trustees who see a need for change may describe what ought to be done to correct the situation. In so doing, they hope to convince skeptical listeners that, compared to what conditions could be, current ones are unacceptable—that efforts to repair matters have been put off too long.

A problem is serious if it represents a danger to the board, the organization it governs, or those served by that institution, for example, if the organization is being disparaged in newspapers, being beaten by competitors, or performing more poorly than previously. Janis (1989) lists a number of conditions that cause members of a board or managers of an organization to realize that a critical problem is developing and should not be ignored:

- Many people among those governed by the board will be unfavorably affected if the situation worsens.

- The efficiency or existence of the institution will be damaged if the situation is ignored.
- Related problems (big and small) contribute to this threat. It will take work to resolve all of them.
- An additional threat is beginning to augment ones already at hand.
- The current threat is clear and unambiguous, not a mirage.
- The situation developed suddenly without much warning.
- There are no established procedures for handling the situation.
- The likelihood is high that the threat and its effects will materialize if ignored. Board members can readily imagine this happening.

Defining the Problem

The problem-solving process begins when a problem is stated for a board and members respond by considering whether the problem is worthy of discussion, that is, whether they ought to work on the problem and, if so, how the discussion should begin. To give weight to the issue, the initial presentation of the problem often includes a description of adverse events that might result if the problem is not resolved. The person raising the question should explain its significance without revealing his or her feelings about it or a preferred solution because a slanted introduction stimulates biased comments from board members. The member presenting the problem explains what information is needed by the board and where it may be obtained so that the board can consider the matter. The person who presents the problem should make clear what kind of action, if any, is needed here and now and what the outcome of an appropriate decision eventually will be.

A problem must be stated clearly because members cannot easily clarify a muddy topic when a discussion is under way. Members usually feel compelled to begin discussing a problem when asked to do so, even if they are not sure what kind of contribution is appropriate and their discussion is accordingly disjointed. Members are embarrassed if they do not know what to say, and they do not like to ask the chair what is going on. Sometimes, the best way to clarify an issue is to diagnose the problem: What caused it?

What barriers have interfered with its solution in the past? Has some deficiency led to the presence of the problem? Often, a sound diagnosis may suggest a solution.

If the central issue is one of choosing from among strongly supported separate positions and it becomes evident that board members are not willing or able to choose among these, it may be wise to change the topic at the outset to one of considering what the criteria are for an ideal solution (Fisher, Ury, and Patton, 1991). What qualities should a best answer have? What interests of members should properly be met by a good outcome? Board members are asked to choose the best among these criteria so they can thereafter use the criteria when deciding which alternative is more suitable.

Identifying Potential Solutions

Once board members accept a problem as worthy of their effort, they begin to think up solutions for the problem. The soundness of the final answer clearly depends on the quality of the ideas developed during this searching stage and the willingness of members to find answers that meet the needs of the board or organization, instead of fulfilling their own selfish yearnings. Because members are more likely to find a better resolution if they have more alternatives to compare, test, and choose from, the climate in a board and the methods members use in identifying potential solutions must encourage members to express themselves freely. Members must often be encouraged to stretch their thinking and generate unfamiliar ways of approaching the issue at hand. Only then will members be able to find creative solutions, avoid settling too quickly upon a likely looking proposal, and avoid starting to evaluate suggestions before that activity is called for.

A discussion leader helps participants overcome three procedural problems that can interfere with the identification of potential solutions. The first is reluctance by members to take part because they fear their ideas will be evaluated unfavorably by their colleagues. The second is members' lack of ideas during a discussion because it delves into topics the members have never considered, which makes them reluctant about expressing their half-formulated ideas. The third is the presence of conditions in the group that restrain ready give-and-take, such as the group being too large for everyone to have a turn, authorities being present who properly should have the floor, or a few members dominating the discussion and leaving little time for the rest to contribute.

Where such situations prevent a board from doing the best it can, responsible members employ methods that reduce restraints to free-flowing discussion. Several useful procedures for discussion leaders are examined next.

Brainstorming. In 1937, Osborn proposed a discussion method called brainstorming for increasing the number of ideas a group may develop during its deliberations. Brainstorming has four basic rules: criticism of one another's suggestions is strictly prohibited, free thinking and wild notions are welcome, numerous ideas are sought, and combination or modification of ideas already offered is in order. Osborn suggested that group members be instructed at the outset on the four basic rules, be allowed to practice the rules, and then be required to follow them. Each idea offered by a speaker is recorded on a blackboard or newsprint pad, and the question for discussion should be as open ended as possible.

Does brainstorming work? The results of research and experience (Camadena, 1984; Diehl and Stroebe, 1987; Fisher, Ury, and Patton, 1991; Forsyth, 1983; Zander, 1985) suggest that the method is most effective under certain conditions. For example, brainstorming works well if after members can think of nothing more to say, they are asked to improve the ideas on hand, with the understanding that criticism of these ideas is now permitted. Brainstorming achieves better results if the group is small (five to eight members), each participant is asked to speak in turn, the atmosphere is informal, and participants are allowed a chance to think about the question privately before brainstorming begins. Among the four basic rules of brainstorming, the prohibition against criticism of others' ideas is the most important. The members of the groups that produce the most ideas during brainstorming sessions like the activity more than other groups and are disposed (on the basis of standardized tests) to tolerate ambiguous situations better than other groups (Camadena, 1984). The best advantage of brainstorming is that members who might ordinarily hold themselves back feel free to take part in a discussion.

Any governing board, when in need of new ideas, can use a form of brainstorming during a regular meeting by temporarily imposing the four rules of brainstorming on the interaction. Members will find that no one person dominates the group's flow of ideas, more members participate than usual, they feel free to offer unusual notions, they develop many suggestions in a brief period of time, no members are "lost in the crowd," and they have fun.

Nominal Group Technique. The nominal group technique is based on research that indicates that people are more productive if they perform a task in the presence of an audience, a phenomenon known as *social facilitation* (Zajonc, 1965). The inventors of this procedure (Delbecq, Van de Ven, and Gustafson, 1975) assume that participants will be more comfortable in offering ideas on a topic needing thoughtful consideration if they have an opportunity to think about and write down what they might say while with individuals who will hear those ideas. The term *nominal* denotes that the participants may actually be strangers to each other, not a true group. In fact, the method is quite useful when a number of people who do not know one another and may be uncomfortable in a meeting come together to develop ideas on an important topic (Moore, 1987).

The technique moves through four steps after the leader states the central question, which is phrased as simply as possible. First, participants write private responses to the question. No interaction is allowed. Second, each person is called upon in turn to offer one of his or her ideas. This idea is posted publicly, and no comment on it is allowed at that time. The ideas of each participant are noted until all ideas have been recorded. Third, participants ask questions about the meaning of any items in the list that are not clear to them. Fourth, participants decide which ideas are the most important and then rank these ideas. The pool of suggestions is then ready for evaluation and a final selection.

Delphi Technique. The Delphi Technique makes it possible for members to offer ideas anonymously on a question that needs better-reasoned answers than they can create during talk at a conference table. It allows participants to comment on ideas proposed by others without knowing who proposed the ideas. The method is especially useful when group members come from different status levels, have different degrees of expertise, or have different levels of power to decide the fate of the people involved. Usually, respondents never meet face-to-face.

The process can take as long as seven weeks, requires several people to run an operational headquarters, and demands skill in asking questions and coding written answers from those running the operation. Some governing boards may see this method as too complicated and slow, but it can provide pooled results no other procedure will provide.

The technique employs a series of questionnaires. The first one contains a small number of open-ended questions and is sent to chosen respondents, who provide answers in writing. The initial questions are devoted to problems, goals, predictions, or requests for objective information. After the questionnaires are returned, the team at the headquarters codes the results and develops a new set of questions in which targeted individuals are asked to comment on main themes among the previous answers. When these questionnaires are returned, new ones are again developed and sent out. This cycle is repeated as many times as is necessary to arrive at a reasonable consensus among participants. Detailed descriptions of the procedure are available in Delbecq, Van de Ven, and Gustafson (1975) and Moore (1987).

This procedure is especially valuable when it is necessary to learn what a specific set of people think about a general issue, future goals, or priorities among alternative activities. It is also useful if disagreement is great or a problem cannot be solved in objective terms but judgments about the issue would help. The only limits to the number of participants are the time needed for coding questionnaires and the cost of mailing new versions of the questionnaires.

Ringi. Ringi is a procedure that is used in Japan when decision makers are stalled or ensnarled in superficialities. Conferees in Japan often do not like to disagree with one another face-to-face. To avoid this discomfort, a written document dealing with the issue at hand and prepared by an anonymous individual is sent from member to member and edited by each in turn without any face-to-face interaction. After each cycle, the draft is rewritten and sent around for further comments as many times as necessary until no more changes are needed and all participants have put their personal seals on the final version (Rohlen, 1975). Some groups find it useful to assign separate parts of a problem to each of several subgroups who prepare an answer for their section. These small reports are then circulated before discussion begins in the larger body.

Deciding on the Best Solution

When board leaders sense that no more alternatives are forthcoming, they turn members to selecting one alternative among those that have been proposed. Members begin to test whether a given approach can resolve the problem and what side effects the approach might have. They consider issues such as the following: What will be the gains or losses for the board or nonprofit organization from each approach? What will be the gains or losses for people served by the organization? How much will members approve or disapprove of their board after if has selected the solution? How will the organization's staff members react to the solution? How will the public react?

When a problem is complex and the effect of its solution is difficult to foresee, the chair of a board should encourage members to break the problem into small steps. Ordinarily, if all goes well, members can agree on which alternatives are the best. However, the path to such an agreement is seldom straight, and the agreement often is the result of bargaining, arguing, and negotiating (Chapter Seven). In addition, members who have more social power usually have more to say in the ultimate decision.

Sometimes, not one of the available alternatives is truly appealing to the board members. In such a case, they may select the least objectionable proposal. If they do so, they will be inclined to explain their choice to themselves and others by inventing arguments in favor of it, a form of rationalizing called *bolstering*. Through bolstering, members try to make their choice appear reasonable by listing favorable consequences that will follow from the decision, minimizing unfavorable consequences, denying adverse reactions, exaggerating the need for immediate action, minimizing the interests of people outside the group, and playing down trustees' responsibility for the consequences following their action (Janis and Mann, 1977).

When a governing board is facing a difficult decision or is making little progress reaching a decision, a skillful leader can move things along by asking members to consider what process they ought to use in working on the problem. To sharpen the discussion about procedure, the leader may ask members to identify the problems that they have in reaching a decision, such as biases among colleagues, incomplete facts, inability to predict the future, rivalrous subgroups, unclear alternatives, or lack of understanding about the cause of the problem under discussion. On the basis of this diagnosis, the leader and the members may devise a way of reaching a decision that will reduce restraints that make them inefficient.

According to Fisher, Ury, and Patton (1991), any decision-making process should have three qualities. First, it should produce a "wise agreement," that is, one that satisfies relevant interests of members as much as possible, resolves conflicts among members, and gives proper weight to the needs of the board and the organization. Second, it should be efficient. And third, it must foster harmony among members.

These authors emphasize that arguing over solutions often leads to poor decisions. For example, when one participant insists that his or her position is best, the individual is locked into that view, increasingly defends it against attack or change, and thus becomes more and more convinced that he or she is correct. "As more attention is paid to positions, less attention is devoted to meeting the underlying concerns of the parties. Agreement becomes less likely" (Fisher, Ury, and Patton, 1991, p. 5). And whatever agreement is reached may be simply a compromise, a splitting of the difference between two beliefs, instead of a sound solution. Arguing over positions also makes a board inefficient because members are tempted to engage in gamesmanship, stalling, threatening to withdraw, or offering minuscule concessions that only slow things down. Arguing over positions "becomes a contest of will" (p. 6) and the ensuing battle may arouse rivalry that spoils harmony among board members.

To avoid unfavorable consequences when board members argue to win support for their preferred solution, Fisher, Ury, and Patton (1991, p. 10) propose a method of negotiation that is "explicitly designed to produce wise outcomes efficiently and amiably." They call this process *principled negotiation,* or *negotiation on the merits.* The method has four elements.

First, people should be separated from the problem. During a heated discussion, participants become emotional and do not think or speak clearly. Often, they become angry and say hostile things to those with whom they disagree. Ad hominem remarks must be forbidden so that people work on the problem, not on each other.

Second, the discussion should focus on participants' underlying interests, not their preferred solution. This requirement recognizes that the object of a decision is to satisfy the reasons people have for favoring a given action. The desires, wants, concerns, and fears behind an individual's preferred solution should be the prime topic of discussion rather than the stated position.

Third, the group should develop and consider many options before making a decision. Participants are more likely to reach a useful agreement if they have numerous alternatives to choose among and can look for the one that best resolves the differences between the interests of the members.

Fourth, the qualities a sound solution must have should be defined. Defining these qualities in advance of discussing solutions allows participants to select a solution that meets reasonable criteria instead of being coerced into accepting a solution that supports the special demands of one or more participants. Another method for evaluating potential solutions is described in Chapter Eight.

Most board members probably believe it is wisest to keep their emotions hidden during decision making. Yet it is hard for members to hide their emotions when a board is dealing with questions involving fairness, justice, morality, or disparagement of the board. Some people believe it is sensible for participants in a discussion to show their feelings freely because their thinking will be enriched by a catharsis.

What best helps a board's effectiveness—if members express their feelings whenever they wish or if they suppress them? Guzzo and Waters (1982) tried to answer this question by comparing the quality of decisions reached by a number of groups operating under one of three instructions. (The topic for each group was the same—justice for a man who was unfairly accused of a crime.) Members in one set of groups were told to express any emotions they felt about the question early in the meeting and at the end of the meeting but not at other times. Those in a second set of groups were told to delay expression of feelings until the end of the meeting, after their group's decision was made. A third set of groups was instructed to avoid any display of emotions while the group was together. A final set of groups, the controls, was given no instructions about showing emotions.

The researchers reported that the highest-quality decisions and the most diverse ideas were developed in groups where members delayed display of emotion until after they had reached a decision. The participants in those groups saw their associates as more effective and energetic than the participants in the other groups did. The groups in which members had an early (and/or late) catharsis came up with fewer ideas than the participants in groups that delayed showing emotion and in the control group, and the members did not work very hard. The groups in which members suppressed all emotions throughout the study fell between the foregoing groups. The results suggest that a group's decisions will be better if participants withhold display of feelings until the end of a meeting. Members thus know they can express anger or strong emotions after the session if they wish.

In another investigation of group processes, Tjosvold and Field (1985) compared the effectiveness of three different styles of discussion while groups were deciding whether a specific individual should be hired by their company. In one experimental treatment, group members were told that their workplace was traditionally a harmonious one, that they should act in accord with that tradition, and that they would be rewarded if their members maintained good relations during their meeting. This treatment was called the *concurrence* condition. In a second approach, group members were informed that their office historically believed in the value of lively conflict among members and that participants should feel free to express their different views as heartily as they wished. In addition, each member was secretly given somewhat differing information about the individual under discussion, thereby ensuring disagreement. This was the *controversy* condition. A third situation, called the *consensus* condition, put participants to work on the issue with no special instructions.

In the concurrence condition, group members were confident about both the quality of the decision they made and their understanding of the issue discussed, even though their exploration of the problem (based on observers' notes during the discussions) was superficial. In the controversy condition, participants were more uncertain about their decision and their knowledge of the issue, even though they probed the question more deeply. Those group members in the consensus condition only examined the issue superficially. Clearly, groups with different styles of discussion differ in their climate and outcomes. Boards have it in their power, it appears, to change the quality of their decision making by changing the way members treat one another.

Irving Janis has studied group decision making in both experimental and natural settings. He based his research on four assumptions. The first is that the value of a decision-making procedure is the major determinant of a successful outcome—good results require good means. Second, most leaders of established organizations know of, and are capable of employing, processes that lead to high-quality policies. But, third, leaders and group members may make no effort to use the most effective methods if they regard the matter before them as having no serious consequence for the group or themselves. Fourth, even when they see the issue as crucial because vital interests are at stake, a condition may arise that causes them to abandon high-quality practices and rely on an unwise way of reaching a resolution.

In his book *Crucial Decisions: Leadership in Policymaking and Crisis Management* (1989), Janis describes the characteristics of a group's process for reaching a high-quality decision when the matter under consideration is important to group members. He lists seven qualities and asserts that every single one of these must be present for a group to reach a high-quality decision. His seven characteristics summarize ideas discussed on the foregoing pages. Janis believes that a successful group member

1. Surveys a wide range of objectives to be filled, taking account of the multiplicity of values that are at stake;
2. Canvasses a wide range of courses of action;
3. Intensively searches for new information relevant to evaluating the alternative;
4. Correctly assimilates and takes account of new information or expert judgments to which he or she is exposed, even when the information or judgment does not support the course of action initially preferred;
5. Reconsiders the positive and negative consequences of alternatives originally regarded as unacceptable, before making a final choice;
6. Carefully examines the costs and risks of negative consequences, as well as positive consequences, that could flow from the alternative that is preferred;
7. Makes detailed provisions for implementing and monitoring the chosen course of action, with special attention to contingency plans that might be required if various risks were to materialize [p. 30].

Implementing the Decision

Members of boards sometimes overlook the fact that their decisions must be implemented, usually by persons other than themselves. The people who are to implement a decision may not do what the board members expected them to do. Therefore, a board is responsible for considering what problems others might have when implementing a decision and what procedures can address these problems.

Other people may fail to implement a board's decision because they received imperfect instructions on how to do so. Or they may demur if the proposed change does not fit what they usually have done; if they do not see the importance of the change they are asked to bring about; if they are anxious about the effects of the proposed change; or if they lack the necessary resources, ability, energy, or time to implement the change.

Because implementation of a decision may arouse the implementer's anxiety, boards often devote attention to ways of winning acceptance for new plans (see Chapter Four). One useful procedure for gaining others' acceptance of a decision is to invite those who are to use the change to participate in making the decision or in helping decide how the decision might best be enacted. Footdragging can be overcome in such a conference by asking group members to identify what procedures will help or hinder their implementation of the change. On the basis of this diagnosis, plans can be made to encourage helpful procedures and avoid hindering ones. Such an approach takes advantage of research that shows that individuals are more likely to abide by a group decision in which they had a part (Cartwright and Zander, 1968).

Conditions That Limit the Quality of Decisions

Several conditions can interfere with efficient decision making by a board. A few of the more common ones are presented here.

Superficiality

If the agenda is crowded during a board meeting, time is limited, or the board members are not very interested in the topic, they may make a decision with a minimum of study. Such rapid-fire methods of making decisions, as Janis (1989) calls them, tend to be hurried, simplistic, and based on generalities. As a consequence, the minimal requirement of good decision making may be absent.

One superficial method of making a decision is to seize upon the members' first useful suggestion (ignoring other possibilities) because this idea seems to solve the problem well enough. Or members may choose a plan that worked in the past because the current problem resembles a problem they solved in the past, fits a point of view that is popular among board members, or has become the standard procedure in similar situations. Dependence on the past is attractive because it requires little effort.

In a third superficial approach, members ask one of their number to examine the problem and inform the rest of the group about it: how to define it, its origin, and an array of alternative solutions. They then make their choice on the basis of this person's briefing. Janis (1989) calls this "the nutshell briefing rule" (p. 40).

Quick-fix methods like these can be useful on minor matters where past experience in using them has been good. But they lead to poor solutions if the problem is complicated and requires clarification before it can be properly discussed and decided. Janis (1989) believes group members are more likely to use superficial methods in solving problems if they underestimate the seriousness of the issue, see an "obvious solution" and grasp it without adequate evaluation, think the problem is too complex for them to understand and therefore try to simplify it, fear a solution will spoil harmony among members, are stimulated by the problem to satisfy personal motives first, or experience strong emotions because the problem seems threatening.

Groupthink

In some cases, board members want to preserve good relations within their group at all costs, so they steer clear of procedures or solutions that might spoil the group's harmony. They put aside good sense in order to find an answer that will help members to remain compatible. Certain kinds of behavior characterize these attempts by group members to maintain harmony. First, the members consider only a few solutions and ignore others. Second, they fail to examine adverse consequences that might follow their preferred course of action. Third, they drop solutions that appear unsatisfactory without examining them well. Fourth, they do not seek the advice of experts. And fifth, they fail to create fall-back procedures in case the chosen solution does not work out.

Janis (1972) points out several ways a board can avoid these behaviors. A board can ask each member to weigh all alternatives critically, request each to discuss the content of their group's deliberations with friends outside the group and to report the results of these conversations, assign the role of devil's advocate to one member, examine the views of people whose ideas are known to conflict with those of the board members, and (once a decision is made) have members consider any remaining doubts at a later meeting.

Unequal Status of Board Members

In some boards, there is a distinct difference in the status of members. For example, in a board for a hospital, nurses may serve along with physicians, or in the board of a professional association, neophytes may serve with world-famous leaders in that field. Individuals who differ widely in their social standing are not always comfortable with one another. High-status group members talk more in the group and direct their comments mostly to other high-status group members. Low-status members talk less and address most of their remarks to high-status members (who tend to think that low-status members talk too much) (Cartwright and Zander, 1968).

A board's leader may find it useful to point out this imbalance when it occurs and to ask high-status members (outside the meeting room) to give more consideration to the contributions of low-status members and to direct more remarks to these members. If such actions do not help the group, the chair may ask members of separate status levels to meet in separate rooms on the assumption that they will talk more freely in those more homogenous meetings. These groups are brought together later to share their ideas. The head of the board need not try to get everyone talking; generally, in a comfortable and efficient group, I suspect that only 30 percent of those present do most of the talking.

Sense of Urgency

When members of a board must deal with an urgent matter, such as the death of the chief executive officer, a fire, a strike, a storm, or sudden and severe criticism of the board, they are prone to make errors when choosing a course of action. Either the pressure of time makes them consider too few options or the problem is given to a small subset of members that does not include experts on the issue. The information available may be untested and biased by the wishes and expectations of those members who seize this opportunity to influence the solution in ways that benefit themselves.

Decision makers who are under stress tend to be less flexible and imaginative than they might otherwise be (Holsti, 1971). In addition, board members are frequently surprised by and unprepared for a crisis. Some farsighted boards try to anticipate emergencies and lay plans for dealing with them should they arise.

Research shows that within a board under stress, members are more willing to listen to one another than to the designated leader. Driskell and Salas (1991) studied group decision making under stress. They hypothesized that members would more often attend to and defer to superior officers during a crisis than during a normal situation in order to place more responsibility in the leaders' hands and ensure an orderly coordination of members' efforts. Instead, they found that members listened to one another more than their leader during an emergency, and there was no tendency for them to defer to authority more than to one another. Low-status members listened to high-status colleagues more during an emergency than vice versa. And high-status participants were more influential than low-status participants in determining the group's plan of action. Apparently, a board employs a familiar form of participative decision making rather than turning to a strong authority for an answer when it faces an urgent question. Chapter Seven considers comparable results in its examination of the behavior of board members during a conflict with another group.

External Criticism

An attack on a board by critics who have a serious interest in that board's conclusions can also interfere with a board's decision-making process. For example, a local board of education debates whether to tear down a neighborhood elementary school and replace it with a new building in a different part of the city. It soon hears from parents opposing the idea who express their views with feeling. The board of a professional society gives its opinion on an issue of public concern (abortion, violence on television, gun control, or ozone depletion) and is attacked by members of its own organization for taking a public stance they deplore.

Critics' comments must be answered when based on incorrect assumptions, even though doing so is embarrassing for the correctors and irritating to the critics, arouses emotional tension, and makes board members advocates rather than dispensers of unbiased knowledge. Advocacy can slow the process of reaching a decision. But criticism may also improve the quality of the decision-making process (see Chapter Nine).

The members of some boards, especially elected trustees, are particularly sensitive to conflicting views of external interest groups. The role of elected trustees is to ensure that the institution they guide serves the interest of the public along with the needs of people who have a special interest in the organization. To perform their duty, members of these boards must know whether the public interest is fostered by the demands of interest groups. If this information is not obvious, the board members cannot be sure which path to follow. The problem becomes more complex if board members are in the midst of a campaign for reelection. In such a case, members must make it clear in board meetings that they are listening to all sides and being fair in their deliberations.

When a decision has been based on the arguments of outside groups, members must demonstrate to those groups that their arguments have been influential. Such displays take time and contribute little to the quality of the discussion or decision, but they reduce the pressure trustees feel. I discuss pressures on a board more in Chapter Five.

Many boards conform to laws that require all meetings to be open. Under these laws, members of the audience must be given an opportunity to comment on questions under consideration. In open meetings, board members tend to keep quiet on matters they would prefer to discuss in a closed meeting, and play to the audience on topics they know constituents support. The presence of an audience can cause biases and distortions in the decision-making process.

The regents for the University of Michigan refused to take part in the appointment of a new chancellor for a branch campus because of the state's open meetings act. As one regent said about the public method of selection, "The best process is one in which the meaningful part can be done in a non-public forum where tougher questions can be asked. . . . Injury is done to the quality of the institution unless we find a way to address the public's right to know and the candidate's right to privacy" (Elgass, 1992, p. 4). Another regent added, "You can ask tougher questions and assess the variety and quality of the candidates if the meetings are not open. That changes considerably if done publicly. To entice individuals, we have to allow them confidentiality all through the process. Confidentiality is of paramount concern" (p. 4).

Short Tenure of Board Members

Boards whose members have had considerable experience working together would be expected to perform better than ones with a brief history or ad hoc groups created to resolve a specific problem. In a study comparing the behavior of members in twenty long-established committees and in twenty groups created anew, the groups made up of veteran members were superior in decision making and in dealing with conflict among members (Hall and Williams, 1966).

If experience improves the ability of a group, it follows that the quality of a group's work might be enhanced when members are taught (by a skilled nonmember) how to make decisions efficiently. To test this notion, Nemiroff and King (1975) conducted an experiment in which a number of groups were told how to deal with differences of opinion among members and how to participate in open discussions while other groups were given no such instructions. The researchers reported that the instructed groups, compared to the uninstructed ones, made better-quality decisions and better use of resources but took a longer time to complete the task. The use of good decision-making processes apparently causes members to be more thoughtful, and thoughtfulness takes time.

Unskilled Board Members

Although a board is greater than the sum of its parts and usually makes decisions superior to those any member would develop alone, it can create better decisions if members are competent. The chair of a board composed of persons with little skill (on either the substantive topic or group process) soon sees that it is difficult to keep participants on the subject because much of what they say is not useful in reaching a solution. My research with a colleague (Zander and Gyr, 1955) showed that members of a board can sense when their solution is not of high quality and are less likely to abide by their decision when they do not think it is a good one.

Larson and LaFasto (1989), as a result of investigating the qualities characterizing effective and ineffective groups, observed that the most successful groups had a majority of competent members. Such members had more of the skills, abilities, and knowledge needed for doing the group's work; greater desire to contribute to that effort; and more capability in working with others than less competent members. The researchers gave the greatest weight to the ability to work well with others.

Summary

Participants on a board often make decisions that require nonmembers to change their behavior or beliefs. Board members can be more certain that such decisions are accepted and implemented by the target people if members identify problems the recipients may have when putting the new plans in place, if members advise the recipients about how to initiate a required change, and if members seek the ideas of nonmembers on the content of the decisions and the methods of implementing the new approach.

Making a group decision is part of a larger process called problem solving. The process usually moves through four stages: defining the problem that requires a response, identifying a number of possible solutions, deciding on the best solution from among the alternatives, and implementing the decision. The results of research and experience suggest that special skills and precautions are needed in each stage. Several procedures are notable as means for increasing the number of alternative solutions: brainstorming, the nominal group technique, the Delphi technique, and ringi. A procedure called principled negotiation is helpful in choosing the best among possible solutions.

A number of conditions limit the quality of decision making in boards, and wise board leaders develop ways of overcoming these conditions. Inhibiting conditions include: use of superficial or quick-fix methods, failure to evaluate ideas on their merit (group-think), differences in the status of members, a sense of urgency during a crisis, attacks on a group by external critics, short tenure of members, or unskilled board members.

3

Key Strengths

Active Participation, Shared Leadership, and Clear Standards

The previous chapters considered three sources of effective behavior in a governing board: board members' motives, a board's mission and goals, and the decision-making process. This chapter considers other behavior that helps determine how well the board functions. Each type of behavior is easy to use, observe, and evaluate. The topics discussed in the chapter are: helping members participate in discussions, sharing leadership of the board, using appropriate meeting procedures, developing clear standards for the board, benefitting from disagreements among members, and selecting appropriate members.

Helping Members Participate in Discussions

During meetings of a board, members spend a good deal of time in discussions where no decision is to be made. Instead, they are educating themselves. Each member integrates others' thoughts with his or her own views about the topic at hand in whatever way seems most sensible. For example, people on the board of a housing community for elderly individuals discuss the significance of new laws for aid to the handicapped, university regents consider recent violations of civil rights on campus, members of a church board examine ways other congregations have helped homeless people, a school board studies the pros and cons of dress codes for students, and directors of a hospital board discuss the significance of a report by the facilities committee.

This type of discussion has three central features. First, members help each other better understand a shared interest or problem but do not try to reach a conclusion. Second, each participant is free to take away whatever ideas he or she finds useful and to ignore the rest. Third, in the long run, the board and the organization it oversees benefit from the development of board members, but this development is not an immediate purpose of the interaction.

A period of discussion serves five purposes for board members:

1. It helps members recognize what they do not know but probably should know.
2. It gives members an opportunity to get answers to questions.
3. It allows members to get advice on matters relevant to the work of the board.
4. It allows members to share ideas and derive a common wisdom on the topic.
5. It allows members to learn about one another as individuals.

A discussion session by board members is not a debate, an argument, or merely a conversation. During a discussion is not the time to reach a decision about action in behalf of the board. Moreover, managing a discussion is not the same as running a meeting on the best solution for an organizational problem because special attention must be given to the discussion's educational and advisory purposes.

To meet these aims, a leader must make sure that three procedural problems are handled well during a discussion session: (1) reluctance of members to participate, (2) members' lack of ideas during the discussion, and (3) conditions in the group that restrain ready give-and-take. This section examines each difficulty separately, even though they overlap to some degree, and considers methods for overcoming each of these problems during a discussion.

Reluctance of Members to Participate

In most discussion groups, one-third of the members do most of the talking. The rest of the members sit silently. Why do some members hold back? Typically, these members know the topic well, so they leave the floor open for members who are considering it for the first time; they are shy and dislike speaking in a public setting; other people in the room have control over their fate, so they avoid contributing or asking questions for fear they will appear inept to those people; they are new members of the group and feel their comments are naive; or they do not u.:derstand the ramifications of the topic, so it has little meaning for them.

The hardest step in starting a discussion is to pose an interesting issue, one that board members will want to work on and will feel they can handle effectively. Too often, a chairperson introduces a subject and is met with silence or a brief response and then silence. Common examples of deadening questions are: What is hard for you to understand in the report? How many clients have we served? Is the CEO's plan better than ours? The first question asks members to reveal their own inadequacies, which is not a popular topic for discussion. The second involves a factual matter and therefore will not invoke much give-and-take. The third asks for a yes or no answer and leaves the direction of subsequent comments unclear. All the questions are somewhat ambiguous, so a member is not sure what kind of response is relevant. Better questions are: In what respects should the report be clarified? Why, as you see it, do clients use our services? In what ways does the CEO's plan differ from ours?

The stillness that follows an uninspiring question can itself be a gentle form of pressure on members to speak, but it will goad them successfully only if the matter before the board is clear to them. A topic must be easy to understand and important and must evoke curiosity if it is to promote useful discussion.

The more meaning a topic has for board members, the stronger their impulse to speak will be. One way to make a topic meaningful is to provide a film, play, excursion, lecture, story, questionnaire, experiment, or role-playing scene related to the topic. When the demonstration is finished, the leader asks group members questions such as: What happened? Why did those things occur? What was most important among those events? Such concrete queries can lead into issues of more direct concern to the board. Whether a lively discussion follows depends on how much the shared experience recalls problems for members and how skilled the leader is in recognizing when participants are absorbed, why they are involved, and what will continue to involve them.

Sometimes it is helpful to begin a discussion by focusing on events that took place in other groups if these events resemble ones within the board's experience. This approach initiates interaction in a way that is not a threat to board members because they analyze the behavior of other people. Discussion flows more easily in such an approach because there are no obviously right or wrong answers. The discussion can eventually lead to identifying similarities between the others' case and the board's situation. Matters may come up for frank appraisal that probably would have been evaded if they had been posed directly.

A familiar way to identify topics that interest board members is to ask for suggestions. Some of the responses may be poorly worded, so the chair should write them on a blackboard, and the participants can then modify the ideas and choose the most intriguing ones. Topics may be worded better if members take time to compose them in writing or if groups of about three members are asked to consider, select, and offer specific issues for discussion. Each subgroup may also appoint a spokesperson who will present the subgroup's opinions.

To create interest in a specific topic, members should be encouraged to think about the matter ahead of time. They can be encouraged to do so if the topic is a main subject of the next meeting. It may be useful to ask members to keep a diary, observe and rate events in the organization they monitor, comment on the actions of colleagues, complete a planned questionnaire on relevant subjects, or interview colleagues about topics that can be considered at a coming session.

Lack of Ideas During a Discussion

The focus of a board's discussion moves from person to person and topic to topic, returning to earlier comments or initiating new branches of thought that are followed or ignored. A discussion leader is often content to let a lively interaction continue without much guidance, even though no clear theme is being followed, because the purpose of the discussion is to benefit individuals with different interests and questions, not the board. The leader should step in, however, when it appears the discussion is dwindling or members want more discipline so they can concentrate on a single issue until they are finished with it.

A board member at a conference table may say little because only one person can talk at a time (or ought to) and others block the member by taking the floor before he or she does. Rapid back-and-forth discussion among members gives a participant little opportunity to plan what he or she might say or to choose what words he or she might use. By the time a member has composed an appropriate sentence, the subject has switched to something else. Each remark by a colleague is, moreover, a distraction to listeners, as they rehearse a statement of their own while following others' talk. Thus, a member in a discussion hesitates to speak unless the member knows what he or she wants to say and feels it is important to insert these ideas into the flow of the discussion.

The group members are an audience for each speaker. They stimulate a person to do whatever his or her dominant inclination is at the moment. For example, if a group member is sure about what he or she wants to say on a given issue, the member states these ideas better in the presence of the other members; the audience stimulates him or her to speak up and speak well. If the member is not sure what he or she wants to say (a different dominant response), the member is less articulate and makes more errors; the audience becomes a source of inhibition (Zajonc, 1965).

Often, a board's discussion delves into topics that members have never considered before, and these unfamiliar issues make members cautious about expressing their views. Therefore, a wise leader develops a way of instilling self-confidence in members so they feel free to offer comments even when their ideas are not fully formed. The leader must, in a sense, provide members with something to say.

One way to initiate discussion on an unfamiliar topic is to divide the board into three or four subgroups and ask each to observe or listen to the same presentation while focusing on different things. The presentation can be a lecture, tape recording, or film, and the three or four separate focuses might be: what the presentation omits but should not, what is not clearly stated in the presentation, what derivations follow from the material offered, and what the practical implications of the ideas presented are. Because each division of the large group takes a separate view of the same material, members in each subgroup see different things. Thus, reporters for each subgroup have something to say that is different from the remarks of people in the other small groups, even though all have viewed or listened to the same material. The contrasts among group reports encourage interaction, efforts to understand, and efforts to correct one another.

A discussion that starts out well may lose its vigor when members run out of things to say and begin to repeat themselves. If so, the chairperson should suggest a new approach, new question, notable differences among members' remarks, or new topic. The chair prepares for this situation by arriving at the meeting with notes in hand, or writing them during the session, about questions that should not be overlooked in the discussion. During slow points in the discussion, the leader can retrace high points in the topics covered thus far or can ask, "Where do we go from here?" Or the leader can summarize the previous content of the discussion in such a way that its main issues lead to the next question. For example, the leader could say, "Why do these things happen?" or "How can we improve matters?"

Participants may need help with process, or the way of interacting, not with the content of ideas. If they are proceeding in a haphazard manner and no topic gets adequate treatment, no one may get much out of the session. Board members can develop awareness about what is wrong in their process and how they might better proceed by appointing one or two people as observers of the meeting. These individuals do not take part in the discussion. They sit at one side, watching how things are being done, not what is being said, and are ready with objective descriptions (not evaluations) of the group's work methods.

Because observers do not take part in the group's interaction, they can study the group's processes as events that affect later events.

As a result, their views are refreshingly different from those of a group member or leader. They might observe, for example, that a few members are dominating the discussion while others who have been trying to have a say are being ignored, the leader allows the discussion to wander without giving any guidance, the discussion needed a summary but none was made, members A and B misunderstood each other but nobody noticed or commented on it, or what C said brought angry responses from members several times. In light of such information, members can consider how they might change their way of working.

A common way to plant stimulating thoughts in a discussion is to ask several participants to present brief prepared statements about opposite sides of an issue at the start of the meeting. These short speeches are stimulating for listeners because the contrasting ideas reveal that there are no perfect approaches and imply that different views are possible. A related method is to ask for brief pro-and-con opinions about the matter at hand. These statements are listed in parallel columns, one column pro, the other con, and members then choose one pair (both a pro and a con) to consider first. Other pairs are then considered.

A useful, yet simple, device is for a leader to request a quiet period of a few moments during which those assembled are asked to reflect silently on questions assigned to them, what has been said thus far, or plans for next steps in the discussion. During this quiet time, each participant gathers personal ideas without being interrupted by the utterances of others. After such reflection, members commonly discover they have new things to say—even though they earlier thought they had exhausted their views on the subject.

Conditions That Restrain Give-and-Take

Some board members may not join in a discussion because barriers, such as authoritative figures or too many people in the group, make it difficult to interact easily or excessive speaking among a small clique of members leaves no time for the rest to contribute.

A speaker with great social power (who may be the chairperson) often says more than all other members combined. This authoritative person makes comments to the group as a whole or in response to individual members who address him or her. A member will more often address remarks to this person than to anyone else. Thus, back-and-forth comments occur relatively less often among members than between this person and a member. A discussion can become a series of two-person conversations to which others at the table listen. The central person is the focus of attention and all who are present seemingly collaborate to make it that way (Bales, 1955; Cartwright and Zander, 1968).

A different kind of inhibition arises when one participant takes more than his or her share of available time. If members value the contribution of this talkative person (he or she is an expert or is greatly admired) and recognize that his or her use of the floor is temporary, there is no problem. But if the person uses more time than is fair or dampens the interest of others, members withdraw. Their withdrawal will become emotionally laden, moreover, if the talkative person wanders, utters useless ideas, or implies that he or she knows more than anyone else and demands to be heard endlessly. Unless modified, such behavior can ruin a board.

I attend a monthly board meeting in which a few members often address angry and suspicious comments to officers or persons giving reports. There is little consistency in the matters they disapprove of or in whom they disparage. But there is much regularity in their style. They make it clear that they are the most discerning members on the board, the rest of us are unaware of what is going on, and the best way they can control our carelessness is to ask needling question or to coerce others into making similar queries. All of us are silently angered after these outbursts, our pace of talking slows down while we suppress a desire to treat the critics as they treat us, we yield to the impulse to be aggressive toward the critics, or several members try to calm things down.

Although many boards are burdened by members who can derail rational discussion, there is little information on how widespread such problems are. Bales (1955) noted, as a result of observing conference groups in real-life settings, that members of the groups were more likely to encourage a state of harmony than conflict. He coded the interpersonal meaning of each comment made in these meetings and reported that participants made twice as many positive comments (agreement, effort to release tension, or

friendliness) as negative ones (disagreement, tense behavior, or un-
friendliness). This ratio was more typical of the more effective
groups. I observed comparable behavior among members of groups
in the experimental laboratory while they worked on tasks requir-
ing close collaboration (Zander, 1971). The number of mutually
supportive actions, such as praising, approving, agreeing, or helping one another, exceeded nonsupportive actions, such as blaming,
derogating, disagreeing, or coercing.

However, hostile remarks often have a greater impact than
favorable ones. Bodenhausen, Gaelick, and Wyer (1978) report that
the purpose behind an angry comment in a group is perceived more
accurately by listeners than the intent behind a positive remark. In
addition, an aggressive statement stimulates an impatient response
more often than a friendly comment generates a favorable one.
Thus, even though hostility may occur less often in meetings than
friendliness, its effects are more likely to be dysfunctional for a
board when it appears (see Chapter Seven).

How can board members deal with an associate's anger?
They must stay calm and cope with aggression as rationally as
possible. A calm attitude by other members keeps the hostility from
spreading through the room and demonstrates to the hostile individuals that their coercive style is in sharp contrast to that used by
others; it is not the tone typically taken by colleagues. While responding to hotness with coolness, members make sure they understand the angry individuals correctly by checking the meaning and
logic of these individuals' statements. ("Let me see if I understand
you correctly, are you saying . . . ?") Listeners also try to discover
what lies behind the hostility. Do the angry individuals perceive
things that the rest have overlooked? What do they hope to gain by
attacking colleagues and their beliefs? Sensible members, in short,
treat others' objections seriously, answer angry members calmly,
and determine the basis of others' suspicions, where these need to
be defined.

As mentioned previously, the size of a group affects how
often a member can talk and how much he or she expects others will
contribute. In a large assembly, a speaker typically must stand to
speak and must use a loud voice. These demands intimidate shy
members and reduce the proportion of members who are willing to

join in the interaction. Another restraint on speech at a board meeting is too little time for what must be done. If the chair often urges speakers to hurry along because the end of the meeting is approaching, members forgo things they wanted to say or talk so fast that the impact of their message is weakened. In contrast, meetings that drag on too long eventually cause members to lose interest.

Interpersonal exchange is more interesting, in the culture of the United States at least, if it evokes different opinions among members. Thus, a leader of a discussion encourages expression of thoughts unlike ones already stated by asking for them or offering them. A constructive argument within a group of learners is valuable because those individuals who hold one point of view hear the opinions of others and modify their own beliefs or feelings when the weight of the evidence convinces them to do so. In an open discussion, in contrast to a decision-making session, participants are less likely to persistently defend their own views or become victims of groupthink because they are trying to learn, are in a mood to modify useless notions, and are willing to help one another learn and modify views.

Although people who listen to a discussion can be learners, most discussion leaders try to weaken barriers against participation so that quiet people will contribute. They assume that these people will learn more by taking an active part than by watching others interact. An experienced discussion leader knows that addressing a question directly to a shy person may pull him or her into the interaction, but this approach can be more frightening than reassuring unless the person is on the verge of talking and cannot find an opening. The leader looks for signs of readiness to speak in the face and posture of a quiet member before calling on him or her. A student will become more ready to respond if a teacher looks him or her in the eye while making a comment. This readiness grows if the teacher listens closely and maintains eye contact while the newly stimulated person is talking.

Participants who speak only to the most powerful group members in an apparent attempt to win their goodwill are not disposed to help others develop new understandings. Indeed, they may see associates as rivals and disparage their ideas. This approval-seeking behavior works against the educational aims of the meeting.

In this case a leader can help by explaining to overeager participants that others need a chance to speak, refusing to recognize
members who have had the floor too often, or mentioning the
things that members sometimes do that cause other members to
keep quiet. The leader may, for example, cite the rules for brainstorming, described earlier, because these illustrate the practices
members might follow in helping one another think and talk cre-
atively. A variation of the protection brainstorming provides for
people who are hesitant to speak is to ask each participant, in the
presence of others, to write a response to a specific issue. These
statements are then considered one by one without revealing their
authors.

Although a discussion period in a board does not end with
a conclusion or a vote, members nevertheless want to sense that they
are moving through separate topics toward an understanding of a
central theme or two, not randomly jumping from item to item.
The person guiding a discussion can forestall members from making disjointed contributions by taking charge at crucial times. He
or she precisely defines the matter under discussion and requires
that comments be limited to that topic only until discussion of it
is finished or interest in it is exhausted. The leader then raises the
next topic and stimulates interest in it before letting interaction
resume.

Two kinds of conditions must be equally present in a discussion if members are to be encouraged to take part: conditions that
foster communication along with creative thinking among participants and conditions that prevent procedural confusion during a
discussion. Each condition must be well developed if a board is to
do its job. Yet each, if too strong, can prevent the other condition
from having its full impact. For example, conditions that foster ease
of communication reduce restraints on members, generate confidence, and create receptiveness to ideas so that members speak
freely. However, such a communication style can promote talk at
cross-purposes or wandering and loss of direction. Leaders who try
to tightly control a discussion reduce ease of communication and
the quality of creative thinking. Thus, these two aspects of leadership can create a circular effect in which each may weaken the effect
of the other. A leader who wishes to create a useful group discussion

must keep the two conditions in balance by using procedures that foster interaction and keep things orderly without inhibiting freedom of discussion. To foster a useful discussion, therefore, an effective chairperson must neither be too free, easy, and accepting nor too controlling and strict.

Sharing Leadership of the Board

Leadership is the performance of acts, by any member of a board, that help the board achieve its preferred outcomes. More specifically, leadership consists of such actions by group members as those which aid in setting group goals, moving the group toward its goals, improving the quality of interaction among members, building cohesiveness of the group, and making resources available to the group. In principle, leadership may be performed by one or many members of the group. Situational aspects such as the nature of the group's goals, the structure of the group, the attitudes or needs of the members, and the expectations placed upon the group by its external environment, help to determine which of these actions will be needed at any given time and who among the members will perform them (Cartwright and Zander, 1968).

The performance of such moves contributes to either of two broad objectives: the achievement of a specific group goal and the maintenance or strengthening of the group itself. A board member is likely to engage in a given behavior, such as offering a summary statement, providing a new suggestion, or making a tension-relieving remark, if he or she is aware that a given action is needed, feels that he or she is able to perform it, and that it is safe to do so. Members more commonly take over leadership actions when several conditions are present, such as the designated leader fails to perform his or her leadership functions, the goal of the group is important to members, participants depend on one another, or a member has experience acting as a leader in another group and knows what is needed (Cartwright and Zander, 1968). Boards do better if leadership actions are provided at the time they are needed, regardless of who provides them.

In many boards, the designated leader tightly controls activities, and few members try to introduce actions for the board. Such centralized leadership may occur if the chairperson resents an effort by a member to introduce a group activity because the chair feels that such a person is trying to steal his or her job. I have seen an angry confrontation between a chairman of a university board of regents and the president of the school over the question of who is to speak first. Likewise, I have witnessed tension between a committee's leader and its secretary when the latter had more good ideas than the former. In other instances, members of a board do no more than listen to the chairperson or answer questions put to them by that person because they do not feel well informed, are newcomers, are low in status, or prefer to have a strong chair. They may want the leader to take care of leadership functions and feel better when he or she does so. Because most boards of nonprofit organizations value the ideals of a democratic society, they perform more effectively, I assume, if their leadership functions are shared among members.

Using Appropriate Procedures in Meetings

When members of a board engage in a series of actions or procedures toward an anticipated outcome, they are employing a group process. We have seen examples of group processes in previous pages.

In Chapter Two, I noted seven actions Janis (1989) believes a board *must* take if it is to reach a sound decision on a problem. Janis assumes that a board can achieve a good outcome only if it uses all these separate group processes. Doyle and Straus (1980) describe a method co-workers might use in a meeting if their superior is present, insists on having his or her own way, and dominates a session. The authors demonstrate that under such circumstances a meeting can be more effective if it uses a process that prevents the superior from running the session. A facilitator is appointed to lead events in a way that ensures everyone has a say. Earlier, I described processes for helping board members collect potential solutions to a problem or to participate freely in a group discussion. Chapter Eight will examine procedures a board may use in resolving a conflict with another unit. A board uses many processes, a specific one in one situation and a different one in a different circumstance. It is helpful to evaluate a given board's action to see if it was appropriate for the current circumstances.

Chapter Two gave examples of inappropriate procedures that were too simple to use in making group decisions. Another inappropriate procedure is one in which a chair conducts a group discussion by asking each person at the table, in turn, to state his or her views on a topic; evaluating the quality of each statement; allowing no interaction among members; and finally describing the "group's" conclusion. In certain circumstances, such a method can be useful but not in most meetings of nonprofit boards. Or a board may become bogged down while discussing a technical problem that members do not understand and that should be referred to an expert for suggestions. Other ineffective procedures include a meeting that goes on after everyone has said what he or she can and the outcome has been obvious for some time or a meeting that is cut short before all had time to say what they had in mind.

An appropriate procedure requires fewer and simpler steps to reach a satisfactory response than does an inappropriate procedure; therefore, it is more direct. It calls for less energy or fewer resources than an inappropriate procedure and therefore is less costly. It also requires less time to complete. Thus, an appropriate activity tends to be a more efficient means for fulfilling a board's objectives than an inappropriate one. The appropriateness of a procedure can be increased if members decide what is to be done and how, under whose direction, and by what deadline.

A board can more easily choose an appropriate process if its purpose is measurable because members who can precisely determine whether the board has fulfilled its purpose can better decide which paths lead to that end. Likewise, they can more reliably select an appropriate activity if the purpose is accessible—that is, if they know which path to take to the goal at the outset.

Developing Clear Standards for the Board

Because board members depend on one another, no member is entirely free to do board business as he or she pleases. Members either conduct themselves as other members expect or are pressed to get back in line. What is the reason for such pressure? What makes this pressure effective? How does a member weaken its impact?

Members of a board commonly agree on qualities they want their board to have, such as pride in the board's performance, skills for the work to be done, smooth collaboration among colleagues, effective procedures for meetings, reasons for their important beliefs, and useful interactions with agents outside the board. Members also try to prevent unwanted conditions within their board, including embarrassment over a poor decision, inefficient procedures in meetings, and unfavorable relations with external agents who make demands of the board.

Members prescribe proper behavior within their board through various policies, regulations, operating procedures, programs, or guidelines. These joint understandings concern the board's way of life and include provisions on, for example, meeting times, duties of officers, procedures for separate tasks, forms for paperwork, expected deadlines, recruitment of members, or cost analyses. They also include requirements of the chief executive officer of the organization the board guides. The board states what specific goals it expects the CEO to accomplish (with the help of the staff), what principles or values the CEO should follow while working toward those ends, and what limits the board places on the CEO's freedom to act (Carver, 1990). I call all of these agreements *board standards*.

To keep the board's standards effective, members must abide by them and require colleagues to do the same. The more important a standard is to the board's health or to attainment of its goals, the stronger the pressure members place on each other to abide by the standard.

A standard becomes significant under two circumstances: members value the condition the standard was established to support and members believe that adherence to the standard will help maintain this condition. For example, the board members of a small college establish policies for recruiting new members. They decide that they will search for individuals who are (or have been) administrators, acquainted with people in important positions, college trained, broad minded, and able to help the school financially. Once the board accepts and implements such standards, they are important to members and will be followed in evaluating nominees, provided that members believe the board needs recruits and that the kind of people described in the policies will help the board.

During meetings of a board, a standard is invoked with such phrases as: "In accord with our earlier agreement . . . ," "As is our practice in this board . . . ," or "I believe the proposed nominee fits our criteria for new board members." Such a reminder of a board's standard justifies the actions being taken or proposed, and if listeners accept the standard, they endorse the action taken in its behalf.

The more important the goal of a standard is to members and the more clearly the procedures are seen as instrumental to the attainment of the goal, the more pressure board members will place on each other to adhere to the standard. If a particular standard serves as a means for maintaining harmony, for example, the more that board members want harmony, the more vigorously they will enforce the standard.

Most boards have a variety of rewards they give to members for adhering to standards. Perhaps the most important of these are indications of approval and acceptance. Since the members of a cohesive board value their membership in the board, they are likely to be sensitive to evidence of acceptance by other board members. Thus, responsible members try to increase the cohesiveness of their board.

If a member's behavior deviates from the board's standards, that member is reminded of the accepted norm and urged to obey it. His or her action is more objectionable to other members and is met with more pressure to conform if the action fosters unwanted qualities in the board and if others think the member will repeat the action. A member whose behavior is repeatedly unsuitable becomes a target of increasingly stronger pressures to change. He or she is urged to give up the offensive behavior and to adopt behavior compatible with the group's policies. Members exert pressure as long as their colleague is still acceptable as a member and as long as there is a reasonable chance of changing him or her. If a target of such pressure does not listen to the board members' admonishments, efforts to correct the member become weaker.

If a member becomes unattractive because of unwillingness to abide by the board's standards, his or her colleagues may consider designating him or her as no longer a member of that body. Avoiding the person, refusing to initiate discussion with him or her, and ignoring points the person makes in a meeting are preliminary steps to such a process, but its ultimate form is more extreme. A board rejects a deviant member by arranging things so that he or she can no longer depend on the group and so that the group need no longer depend on that member—the conditions of belonging are abolished.

Many boards have no formal means for removing a member. In such a case, members must tolerate deviant behavior, create procedures for formalizing expulsion, or make it likely that the nonconforming member will drift away from the group by giving him or her marginal duties that reduce the individual's impact on the board. Deviant behavior may be overlooked if the maverick is valuable to the group, has a high-status position on the board and in the community, or has served the body well in the past. The member has earned what is called "idiosyncrasy credit" (Hollander, 1958). Members ignore an associate's unconforming acts if they are not attracted to the board themselves and thus do not care to defend its standards.

A board's standards can have good or bad consequences. The standards are good for a board if they provide convenient rules for actions so that the board does not have to invent a procedure to follow every time it takes up an accepted duty. Thus standards can help make the board efficient. Standards help members cooperate easily because each member knows what others are to do for the health of the whole. Standards define ways members ought to behave so that their board will survive and serve their organization and the community well. Standards delineate what interests are important to the board and deserve attention. And standards spell out policies to guide the actions of the chief executive the board monitors and, in turn, his or her staff.

Standards can have a dark side. Whyte (1957) says that standards make members of an organization unable to resist its every demand. According to Whyte, members' peace of mind requires them to surrender and adopt the requirements of the group, and in doing so, they lose precious personal qualities. Other researchers point to the difficulty an organization has in introducing valuable changes that differ from established standards (Lippitt, Watson, and Westley, 1958; Rogers, 1983; Rothman, Erlich, and Teresa, 1976; Zander, 1990). Members hold on to a given standard in the face of pressures to transform it from outside the board because they fear colleagues will reject them if they agree to a shift, or they are uneasy about a future without the structured organizational life standards provide. Nevertheless, changes caused by new technologies, mores, laws, or beliefs make it evident that members at times need to accept new ways. Governing boards are more likely than other groups to recognize such a need if they believe that a major part of their mission is to plan for the future of the organization their board oversees and to introduce new ways when that seems wise.

Organizational consultants can help boards introduce change efficiently. Many of these specialists operate on the assumption that a change can best be introduced into an organization by helping all members arrive at a new consensus at about the same time. Resistance against accepting a different view, which may arise because no member will accept a change until he or she knows how others feel about the matter, is prevented by giving relevant persons a say in the transition, a chance to express support for or against the change, and the means to take part in implementing the shift in collaboration with others (Lippitt, Watson, and Westley, 1958).

Benefiting from Disagreements Among Members

Board members differ now and then in their expressed opinions, but such differences seldom become arguments because those who differ are usually testing one anothers' views while searching for a view they can jointly accept. Several conditions help members benefit from their conflicts. One of these is a disposition among members of boards of nonprofit organizations to maintain a sense of harmony. The other is the tendency among members to resolve differences in a constructive way.

As noted earlier, I assume that members of a board are more disposed to foster a state of group harmony than a state of discord. I also assume that harmony is more easily maintained if members are alike in their hopes, ambitions, and goals for themselves and the board because then each member knows what to expect from the others and why a particular member acts in a certain way. Colleagues' actions are also more acceptable when they are directed toward accepted ends.

Members tolerate dissonance on the board if they recognize that they can benefit from considering contrasting views; disagreements that lead to agreements are good for the group. Members may also tolerate disagreement over how they can implement a demand made of them by external persons who have a right to put pressures on the board.

Disagreements become unpleasant to members, however, when the disagreements are unresolvable, colleagues are unwilling to engage in a joint task because of the disagreements, rivalrous groups are formed that support separate views, members refuse to accept assignments, or members disparage the board and its efforts to do its duties. Fortunately, such events within a board usually stimulate attempts to regain harmony.

A conflict exists within a board when two parties disagree over what the other should or should not do. A conflict gets much of its intensity from the "shoulds" and "should nots" put forward during discussion. Each side "knows" what ought to be done or said and "knows" the opponent is wrong. I have seen conflicts arise within a governing board because of unwillingness among some members to accept individuals nominated for the board, different views about allotment of funds to departments, disagreement between the president of the board and the chief executive officer over who should speak for the organization, contrasting ideas about how to apply for a grant from a government agency, separate beliefs about how to settle a lawsuit, doubts about a plan to create a new office in order to attract a valued person to the staff, or feelings among a clique of members that the rest of the board is ignoring the needs of one department.

Members who disagree with one another tend to talk with each other exclusively and allow little space for bystanders to intervene. Neutral members recognize what is going on and refrain from talking if the discussion is a good one on a central issue. If the disagreement is on a tangential item, however, and appears to be a waste of time, responsible members should intervene and ask the members who are in conflict to settle their differences elsewhere. The conflict is thus resolved by pushing it aside.

Some conflicts within a board are productive, others are not. Witteman (1991) suggests that a useful conflict, in contrast to a useless one, generates more

- Ideas among members
- Critical evaluation of ideas offered within the group
- Widespread participation throughout the membership
- Flexibility of ideas and actions by members
- Efforts to summarize the direction of the discussion
- Activity intended to reach a conclusion
- Widespread influence from member to member and from members to the leader
- Agreement among participants

If some members are in heated disagreement on a matter that deserves settlement and no resolution is at hand, neutral members may try to resolve the conflict. If they do so by joining the discussion, seeking to hear and understand both sides, the initial confrontation may simply become more intense. Each supporter of a given view argues for the correctness of his or her approach and ignores comparable pronouncements from rivals. As a result each becomes more convinced that his or her ideas are superior—the individual likes the sound of what he or she is saying.

As the people on the two sides become more attached to their positions and more eager to defend the positions, their rationality dissolves and they display hostility in their manner of expression. Whatever one side does while trying to coerce or threaten the other is copied by the people to whom it is directed. These displays of strong emotions heighten the conflict; as people on each side speak, they use stronger language and the anger escalates. As the argument intensifies, people on each side refuse to believe anything that those on the other side say or do and make no attempt to understand the rivals' comments. Both sides want to win, not work toward a best answer—they already think they know what the best answer is.

Eventually, the tension in an argument begins to flag as bystanders make it clear that the disagreement is unpleasant to them; is not settling the issue; and is displaying behavior that is not accepted, approved, or used by colleagues. Also, the emotions of those in conflict cannot remain at a high level for a long time. These individuals begin to listen to peacemakers who urge them to return to a rational discussion.

The peacemakers are most effective if they encourage those involved in the disagreement to state what interests lie behind their insistence that a given behavior or belief be accepted and suggest how the arguers might fulfill these hidden desires in ways other than insisting on the correctness of their point of view. As noted in Chapter Two, rational problem solving can be encouraged among people who support different solutions to a problem. An effective board may help subsets of members resolve an argument. If it cannot do so, the board must live with whatever answer is imposed on it by the most influential supporters of a given view.

Selecting Appropriate Members

The members of a board are chosen in different ways: by the public at large, by people who belong to an organization managed by the board, by the organization's chief executive officer, or by a nominating committee that proposes names to the board for its approval. Regardless of who selects board members or how, those people who have a say in choosing the members know that some individuals are more suitable than others for a given board and try to discern who is best among the candidates.

The people who select board members judge what conditions the board and (indirectly) the organization it monitors need to foster. Does the board need members who will bring with them new influence, prestige, wisdom, energy, experience, behavior, contracts, or trustworthiness? Does the board as a whole need more pride in its performance, financial support, members, talent, collaboration, effective procedures for its work, or interactions with agents outside its boundaries? People who choose board members must understand what changes a board requires before they begin recruiting because these requirements serve as criteria of appropriateness when deciding which candidate best meets the board's needs.

During the selection process, a potential recruit may need to be convinced that he or she will find satisfaction from membership on the board. The recruit must understand that he or she will help the organization or community by joining and will have opportunities to do things he or she values, such as use talents, practice his or her profession, accomplish personal goals, have fun, win approval, be personally changed, or work with compatible persons.

Careful selection processes help a board add members who become committed to it and who value their membership. Groups that favor the recruitment of individuals who are "like us" hold their members longer and have more stability, partly because the similarity in members' beliefs and style generates harmony. Also, a careful selection process usually generates new members who do not need to be heavily pressured to conform to group standards because they accept the need for regular procedures and limits.

What personal characteristics are most useful in the members of a decision-making entity like a board? Larson and LaFasto (1989) studied the criteria used by people who choose members for three different kinds of teams: problem solvers, creators of new objects or methods, and task performers. They reported that problem-solving groups (like boards) want and have better success with members who are intelligent, wise in ways of the world, sensitive to the needs of other people, and high in integrity. Groups that perform physical tasks, in contrast, want members who are action oriented, committed to the goals of the group, loyal, and responsive to the demands of their situation and who accept a sense of urgency.

Janis (1989) says there is little evidence that individuals with one kind of personality are better decision makers in a group than those with a different kind. But he believes research will eventually show that people with the following qualities are more prepared to hear what others say and to offer their own ideas in a problem-solving setting:

- Conscientious and attentive to cues that function as warnings for their board
- Open, imaginative, willing to act independently, and willing to change routines when that appears to be necessary
- Able to be stirred by events, not steadfastly cool and detached from the effect of pressures
- Realistic about their organization's stability and vulnerability

- Confident of their ability to do what is necessary as a member of a board
- Free of a need for constant approval by others
- Not having a strong wish for power or superior status
- Undaunted by ruthless behavior among critics who demand that the board change things at once
- Not persistently negative or hostile toward their organization or holding the belief that the group deserves disloyalty
- Able to remain calm in response to provocations by advocates who appear before the board

The criteria suggested by Larson, LaFasto, and Janis can remind members of qualities their board might need, or should avoid, when nominating or voting for new members.

Summary

Responsible board members enhance the effectiveness of their board by ensuring that several processes are performed well.

- They make it possible during open discussion periods for members to overcome fear of participating, discover things they wish to say, and break through barriers that inhibit their readiness to talk in a meeting.
- They encourage designated leaders of the board to welcome the performance of acts by any member that help the board achieve its objectives, that is, share leadership of the board with colleagues.
- They employ procedures in meetings that are appropriate for the task to be performed.
- The develop standards that maintain qualities members want the board to have and that can be changed when necessary.
- They create conditions in the board that foster harmony among members.
- They are aware of and welcome conditions that generate harmony on the board and help members resolve disagreements in a constructive way.
- They choose new members who are most competent and appropriate for their board.

Part Two

How Boards Work Effectively with Constituents

4

Grass-Roots Support
Gaining Constituent Backing for Board Decisions

On crucial concerns, more than on minor ones, members of a board recognize that they should explain to the community what they are doing, so as to forestall uninformed external opposition to their actions. How do they go about winning acceptance of changes they wish to put in place?

Motivating Constituents to Accept a Board's Decisions

When board members decide to introduce a different practice they must assure others that the new plans are useful and worthy of acceptance. Those people affected by the new practice may go along with it for any of several reasons. They may think that conforming will win the approval of people interested in their behavior. They may admire the way those on the board think or act and may want to behave as they do. They may see the proposal as a requirement they ought to fulfill since the board has the right to place demands on them. Perhaps they believe they will be pleased by the results of the suggested action. They may see the proposal as an opportunity to help disadvantaged clients. Or they may be convinced that the transition is sound and should be supported so that the organization remains effective, even if the change has unfavorable effects on some individuals (French and Raven, 1959).

Most board members understand that people who will be affected by a given change want to know what the consequences of the shift will be. So the board members attempt to reassure the targeted individuals. For example, trustees on a church board propose to its staff and congregation that the membership try to help the homeless. They first get listeners to care about the fate of the homeless ("Many of them never get a square meal!"), and they then describe the satisfaction churchgoers will develop while on this mission: churchgoers will be proud of their compassion, touched by the gratitude of the homeless, and feel less guilty about the condition of the homeless.

The rule board members are following in taking such an action is this: the stronger the motive or desire that board members arouse among listeners and the stronger the chances that this motive or desire will be satisfied by what the trustees propose, the more members of the board will influence the views or behavior of the listeners. In accord with this rule, board members strengthen a relevant motive or desire in listeners by making it salient to them, or by helping them recall the value they placed on this wish in other settings, and by showing them that attainment of the proposed objective will give them satisfaction.

Not all boards operate by this rule. Indeed, some adopt no strategy at all to motivate others to accept change because they assume that whenever they speak, listeners will suppress questions, bury their doubts, and do what they are told.

When the influence of board members depends on the motivation of those they hope to change, board members can take any of several practical steps. In general, they tell interested people about the need for a change and try to motivate them to want or accept the change.

Board members try to discern what is most important to those they wish to influence by observing them in action, talking to them about their satisfactions or frustrations, making tentative proposals and watching their reactions to these, or asking members of other boards how they influenced similar groups. Once a specific desire has been stirred in a targeted group, board members elaborate on the value of satisfying it. They emphasize that implementation of their proposal will result in consequences the individuals prize and that the change being sought is not for the benefit of the board. Board members encourage the individuals to take proposed steps by assuring them that they are competent to do so and build their confidence by providing them with needed resources, relevant skills, and useful procedures, while arousing their willingness to try a new way of doing things.

Board members then call for action and an end to talk, study, or waiting. They press for a date when the change is to be introduced, propose a schedule, and continue urging until the change is in place. Trustees do these things when creating readiness in others to accept a change because they recognize that merely asking for a shift is often not enough; they must also counter forces that point in the opposite direction. If restraining forces are not weakened, the pressures to change may result in increased uncertainty among those being addressed but not in an enduring change (Cartwright and Zander, 1968).

Involving Constituents in Changes Initiated by a Board

Most boards have a mixed audience: a chief executive officer; employees; and individuals with a vested interest in what the board does, such as clients, students, or members of the board's organization, neighborhood, or community. People in any of these groups may applaud or protest a board's action.

If trustees believe it is inappropriate for them to issue orders, threaten painful penalties, offer a reward, or bargain with those they wish to influence and believe it is more sensible to help people see the satisfactions that can be derived from a specific change, how do they make their proposal acceptable? Often, they interest targeted groups in a change by giving them a role in defining the kind of change that might be made. By doing so, the board members ensure that the others' motives will arise from the value of the change itself, not from rewards or threats offered by the board.

Board members can give nonmembers a chance to participate in the board's planning process through five procedures. In describing these procedures, I begin with ones that require little listening by the trustees and proceed to ones that require increasing collaboration by board members and constituents.

Which of the methods board members use when trying to make sure their actions are accepted depends upon three considerations: how well the method works in attempts to interest or influence others, how well it suits the purpose and values of the board (or those governed by the board), and what kind of satisfaction it will bring to board members and people affected by the board.

Taking No Direct Action

One method of involving nonmembers in a board's planning process simply concentrates on helping others become aware of an undesirable state of affairs. Board members talk among themselves about what is wrong and speculate about what could be done to improve the situation. They leave the topic without a resolution or an agreement to discuss it again. They assume that minutes of the meeting or news of the discussion will reach people who already have an interest in the issue and that these people will come forward with useful ideas or encouraging words. Or a board might try to define an enduring problem more precisely than in the past by asking questions such as: Are our costs really out of line? Are we getting the kind of attendance we want? Is attendance low downtown because too few people work in the area? Are all students angry or only the few who allege everyone is upset? Are citizens' objections to noise in libraries warranted?

Why would board members postpone decisive action in this way? Perhaps their thinking on the matter is ill defined, so they talk about it long enough to make the issue clear to themselves and to determine if they ought to give the topic more attention. Members may believe that observers know more about the problem than they do themselves, so they try to increase the willingness of others to make suggestions. They may dislike the groups who will benefit from a solution and may prefer not to provide rewards to them. Members may believe they should not talk about the problem publicly until sure what they want to do because a weak or poorly formulated plan can needlessly stimulate opposition. They may put off treatment of the difficulty because they expect that open discussion at this time will be taken as a sign of weakness.

The usual outcome of this approach is silence; if people who might be interested in the matter do not hear about board members' interest, few of them will pay attention to what the board does. Some people may be too uncertain about their opinions to tell board members what they think. Those who do approach the board about the issue will be deeply concerned with it, are self-motivated, and feel something should be done.

Why is this method effective? It gives constituents a sense that this is their chance to speak up, to get in on the matter early. These people know the issue well, so their ideas can be helpful. They are aware of the satisfactions they seek. Above all, they come forward on their own, not because they are urged to do so.

A board can influence nonmembers even though it does not meet with them or address them directly. Board members may adopt a stand-aside approach because they dislike interacting with targeted groups, fear the consequences of interacting with them, or recognize that the strongest motives are ones people develop on their own. This method is most effective if board members make it known they suspect the issue deserves attention and that they will listen to those who have proposals.

Providing Models of a Potential Change

Board members can stimulate the interest of those people they intend to influence by providing models of a potential change. The board members demonstrate a possible solution or several options instead of meeting with those they want to reach because they assume that providing a model will intrigue observers and inspire them to ask questions, offer ideas, or adopt the model. For example, a board of regents sent faculty members to a nearby university to observe that school's laboratory procedures for research on virulent contagious diseases. The faculty members later gave the regents their views about these procedures. Models or exhibits have been used to show interested citizens what a new hospital will look like, central features of a proposed new program, the uses of money gathered by a United Fund, and what new landscaping can do for an old building. A board may provide a demonstration of how its meetings will go if the board members follow a different procedure in presenting reports and in hearing from the audience.

Why do board members choose to provide models of potential changes? Providing models is a comfortable way to furnish information that does not require contacts or embarrassing confrontations with constituents. The use of models can be a sound teaching method if the people to be influenced are looking for ideas and interested in a demonstration. A field trip can arouse a desire for change if it demonstrates that people in other places handle a common problem more sensibly than local citizens.

A demonstration or a model is effective, of course, only for those people who get to see it and who find it attractive or stimulating. A model must provide a visible good example, have clear and appealing features, and be shown to people who might approve of it. A model's impact is increased if many people in the general public praise it and make their feelings widely known. A model can be effective when those shown a model wish to contribute ideas about an action the board is considering.

Providing General Information

Members of some boards try to win interest in potential actions by giving information to stakeholders and anyone else who will listen. They do not try to persuade the audience, they merely give information about problems or steps that might be taken to solve problems. They try to show audience members that things may be ripe for a change or that a given move is sensible. They distribute this information on the assumption that some people it reaches have an interest in the issue and are looking for ideas that will help them understand it.

Information can be provided to an audience through newsletters, special meetings, classes, conferences, memoranda, speeches to clubs, workshops, posters, and so on. Members of a board provide information for several reasons. First, they think their audience wants the information. Second, they assume the audience will judge the information to be unbiased and reliable because it comes from the board. Third, they know it is desirable to get their ideas to as many people as possible because the recipients have a vote or a vested interest in the board's plans and the board needs the support of many people. Fourth, giving information does not necessarily require face-to-face meetings with people whom the board would like to avoid. It is an anonymous approach or can be. The procedures to be employed are clear, even though they demand some skill, and outside help can be hired if necessary. This method is preferred by board members who want to be sure that other people have the necessary facts.

Most people exposed to information given out by a board ignore it. Two kinds pay attention: those who are looking for an answer to the problem and find it in the data provided and those who have ideas on the matter and discover that information confirms views they already possess. People who never have dealt with the issue and have no ideas about it may be drawn to the information if the style used by the presenters is particularly attractive, agreeable, and trustworthy. The information will have a stronger impact if it speaks to a need of the listeners and suggests a means whereby that need can be fulfilled. Information is most effective if it proposes an objective in clear terms, indicates what must be done to reach that end, suggests a plan of action, and assures targeted groups that many other people who are interested in attaining the goal will help in efforts to reach it.

Instructing a Chosen Population

A board may decide to help particular people learn things that can help these people or their colleagues perform better. For example, a computer system may be introduced into a library, hospital, or school that has been collecting and analyzing data by other methods. To use the computers effectively, certain procedures within an organization have to be changed. These new procedures are taught to selected individuals who then teach others what to do. After initial training, many individuals will figure out on their own how they can make the best use of the computer on their job. These individuals are given autonomy in working out new procedures because they know their roles better than an adviser does.

An illustration of this method of influencing people is given by Rogers (1983), who studied how it is used among farmers. The teaching begins when a trainer selects a set of farmers in a neighborhood and shows them a new procedure, such as drip-watering of cherry trees. This group meets several times to learn both the theoretical and practical sides of the innovation. The trained farmers then apply what they have learned to their own farm (if they wish to do so) and make the results of the new procedure visible to neighbors by using the new procedure on only a part of each field. The effects of the new method and of its absence can be seen by neighbors as they pass these fields. The farmers using the innovation welcome questions from passersby. Modeling and neighborly discussion of the new practice are central parts of the diffusion process. By means of these over-the-fence conversations, the information is radiated widely. Observers work out a way to use this information in their own fields if the demonstration before their eyes interests them, or they ignore it.

Rogers (1983) has studied the steps a change agent typically takes when encouraging the adoption of a new practice. The change agent

- Shows potential adopters that their current practices are not wholly satisfactory and could be improved
- Tells a selected set of listeners about new procedures available to meet their needs
- Helps listeners identify the causes of problems in their own situations
- Assists people in defining the best solutions for their particular difficulties
- Gets people to commit themselves to a method that appears to be a remedy for their situation
- Aids committed individuals in their efforts to translate this new plan into action
- Follows up with each learner in later months to be sure the new practice is working and to help him or her establish a continuing routine
- Terminates the relationship between teacher and student when it appears the latter can handle the new method alone

To use the above steps effectively, Rogers (1983) says that the people chosen for the initial training sessions have to be selected carefully. They should be interested in new ideas, better educated than most people in the group, willing to try new methods, and naturally friendly and sociable. The people these newly trained trainers would reach are influential individuals who will adopt new ideas if doing so does not cause them to forgo the benefits they get from the way they now do things. The individuals serve as gatekeepers who open the way to new practices in their department, neighborhood, or agency. When they adopt a given process, it is more likely to be accepted by others nearby than if the innovation were taken up by individuals with little power.

This way of making a change acceptable is used for several reasons. The modification being advocated by members of the board is based on evidence or knowledge that targeted groups do not possess. The new information is from data accumulated by the organization itself, experts in the field, or scholars. Board members recognize that these ideas will be helpful to those who receive them and that their application will differ from place to place. The targeted individuals will use their training more readily if they have freedom to use it as they wish and advice is available if needed. Some listeners will be eager to learn about the proposal and to serve as advisers or demonstrators. Colleagues learn from colleagues and do so by trying to improve conditions in their own activities. No one presses anybody to do anything.

Using Joint Problem Solving

In joint problem solving, people from two or more groups work together to find a suitable course to follow. Neither side openly intends to demand that its point of view be taken as the final outcome. Both groups wish to have a say and to influence one another while working toward a product that each can accept. Their cooperative goal is to find a wise solution, even if doing so puts some people at the conference table at a disadvantage (Deutsch, 1973).

If board members agree to joint problem solving or ask a subgroup of the board to be involved in the process, they admit that things need improvement, that neither the board nor the staff has a complete answer, and that people governed by the board or its clients have useful ideas that should be considered when seeking a solution. Board members give up some of their legitimate power when they agree to work with the views of constituents. The actions involved in effective problem solving, presented in Chapter Two, also apply here as long as the two parties are not in conflict and wish to move toward a sound solution.

A joint approach to problem solving works best if the board members and the people they work with value rational behavior, know how to act in a collaborative setting, and are confident they can handle the procedure well. The procedure can work well because the people the board invites to help in considering the issue feel they can speak to the issue honestly and need not defend themselves from retribution by the board if what they say does not please board members. All parties willingly seek the best answer and accept what they find, even if it is not what they initially favored.

Joint problem solving is most useful if a good solution could be one of several alternatives, each of which needs to be evaluated. Participants will be satisfied with a joint decision if they welcome the result and feel confident that their action will be acceptable to others. If the process they employ is awkward and inefficient, however, or if others' needs have been ignored, the group's product will probably be poor.

Dabney Park (1990) believes that decision making is more difficult for the board of a nonprofit organization than for the board of a business because a nonprofit organization has no stockholders to provide guidance, as does a company. Instead, its "decisions result from the interest and influence of people on the organization's board and staff" (p. 1). These people have to build understandings, agreements, and commitments, which is complicated to do if the board has the power to make decisions on its own without considering the views of staff members and constituents.

Preventing Misunderstandings of a Board's Decisions

Members of a board want to be sure that their actions are understood by those who feel the effect of the actions. To this end, they may do three things. First, board members inform themselves about ideas constituents have on topics the board is considering. They learn about the others' views because they will make better decisions if they consider more options, and stakeholders are more likely to concur with a board's decision if the board examines the opinions of those who wish to be heard (Fisher, Ury, and Patton, 1991).

Trustees may use several methods to discover what others think, including:

- Holding a public meeting to ensure that all sides have a chance to speak
- Inviting people with special knowledge about the issue to talk at a meeting so they will not miss this chance to state their beliefs
- Seeking out opposing views among those who ought to be heard but do not volunteer themselves
- Inviting organizations with a special interest in the matter to send representatives and present the opinions of their group
- Asking established committees of the board to describe views they have heard or developed on the subject
- Conducting forums on the future of the organization, in which members of the audience speak on the broad topic, a panel treats issues in need of airing, or small groups are created to foster easy discussion of the stated problem

Second, members of a board ensure that those with an interest in a topic before the board are well informed about this topic. People who have a stake in a given problem may not learn in a timely fashion that it is being considered by the board. If they knew the matter was coming up, they would be more likely to attend a board meeting on the issue and more able to offer considered views to the board and the organization. People who suspect they are being denied information may become suspicious that the board is hiding things.

Trustees may use several procedures to ensure that others are informed on a topic, including:

- Arranging to have an organizational newsletter describe the pros and cons on the issue before the board
- Encouraging relevant groups to send observers to meetings of the board, who then report to their colleagues

- Discussing a controversial topic at two or more meetings before a decision is made
- Making the trend of their discussions publicly known between these two meetings

Third, members of a board help nonmembers inform themselves about recent actions by the board or about issues coming before it soon. Board members can easily keep themselves up-to-date on current matters, but other individuals need help in discovering the details of a crucial problem. Well-informed people will base their comments or questions on facts, rather than fears, misinformation, or false assumptions.

Observers of a board often wish to gather information on their own. Accordingly, board members can make it known that critics have permission to look into books, records, or other sources to learn what they can about the background of the issue; there are no secret files or conspiracies. In addition, they tell others where to find information they wish to examine. They make it known that people with an interest in the fate of the organization have a right to express their views to the board and to hear the views of others.

A school board, which must put its budget up for a vote by local citizens, is an example of a public body that tries to help nonmembers stay informed. Bendiner (1969) writes that members of a school board spend many hours trying to win approval of a forthcoming budget by circulating throughout their town, explaining the budget, and reassuring voters that the funds are necessary and will be spent wisely.

The directors of hospitals realize they can win wider acceptance by employees of measures to control costs and evaluate quality if they require that clean-up crews, nurses, and physicians all take part in determining the size of the budget (Brown, 1976). This is an excellent way, according to Brown, to help staff members recognize sources of costs that have to be restrained by those who take care of patients. Physicians, who visit a hospital for a brief time each day, may not be aware of how care can be provided less expensively. Inviting physicians to take part in budget setting, says Brown, makes them more prudent in the orders they write.

Summary

A board's decision will affect many people who want to know what the change might mean for them. So trustees try to show questioners that the plan will satisfy them by arousing salient motives among listeners and demonstrating that the board's proposed change will meet those desires.

Board members often try to help constituents be involved in a specific change. Five methods are useful here: board members discuss the problem at a meeting but make no decision, provide public models of an appropriate solution, offer general background information, teach chosen individuals how to implement a new procedure, or join with listeners in a problem-solving session to evaluate or improve the board's plans. Board members can make sure their proposals are not misunderstood by informing themselves about others' views, making sure listeners understand a new plan, and helping listeners inform themselves on the topic.

5

Staying on Course
Responding Effectively to Social Pressures and Legal Constraints

The actions of a board or the organization it governs can cause uneasiness among nonmembers. For example, a school board may allow unsafe buses to be used in transporting students, stall the integration of schools, or hire poorly trained teachers. The board of a hospital may ignore complaints of unsanitary procedures in its building. The board of a condominium may not approve of repairs to living quarters requested by residents. Because boards or their organizations may make moves that alarm or harm others, their actions are closely observed by nonmembers. Some of these observers, such as parents, citizens, clients, or others interested in the actions of a board, exert social pressures in urging the board to change its practices. Other observers are lawmakers or members of legal regulating agencies who enact rules that limit a board's activities.

Social Pressures from Concerned Citizens and Groups

Bendiner (1969) outlines the many groups placing pressure on boards of education: parent-teacher associations, fans of the school's sport teams, interest groups wanting lower taxes, politicians, owners of business firms, influential citizens, friends of board members, old-line families, church groups, labor unions, chambers of commerce, service clubs, welfare organizations, the League of

Women Voters, teachers' associations, and political parties. Sources from outside the community include the state's department of education, various state agencies, bodies that give federal aid, foundations that grant funds, educators' associations, college registrars, and suppliers of school equipment.

What do these influencers want? Teachers, for example, ask for a part in union bargaining sessions or a say in setting policies for the system because they are professionals and believe they can make sounder decisions than those made by the amateurs on their board (Zeigler, 1964; Bendiner, 1969). They try to change the views of board members on maintaining decorum in the school cafeteria, salaries, procedures used to settle grievances, or details in their contracts. If their union is powerful, teachers may even convince the board to commit funds it does not have, making it necessary for the decision makers to request an increase in the school tax. A school board may be more open to emotionally expressed pressures than boards of other kinds of nonprofit groups because parents declare, with feeling, that they want schools to take on difficult projects, such as protecting their children's safety and ensuring their offspring a successful and happy life.

A developing source of pressures on school boards is a national organization called Citizens for Excellence in Education. This group is "dedicated to restoring prayer in the classroom, banishing anti-biblical language and teaching the story of creation in science classes" (Nazario, 1992, p. A1). It works toward these ends by supporting candidates in school board elections who favor its ideas. According to Nazario (1992), the organization claims to have successfully backed the elections of 1,965 school board members, intended to elect 3,100 more in 1992, and is marching toward its goal of "owning" a majority of the members on all 15,400 school boards in the United States. Since 1989, it has developed 925 community chapters, which apply pressure on their local school board. The eventual aim of this body, some critics believe, is the replacement of public schools by religious ones.

Regents of universities also face social pressure—from faculty members, students, parents, and alumni. They also are exposed to vague and shifting requirements of federal agencies and accrediting bodies and the whims of legislators or wealthy patrons.

For example, a national agency that stands behind student loans urged universities to curb students' political actions that it found distasteful on pain of losing financial aid for students. Most boards of regents ignored these threats (Holmes, 1969).

Regents find that policies they crafted a few years ago because of social pressures are no longer acceptable and have become problems rather than answers. For example, students rioted a decade ago when urging their colleges to recruit minority students. Today, some students disparage their minority classmates. Students also rallied in the past to obtain greater freedom of speech. Today, many students do not speak publicly on social issues for fear they might say something that is currently unfashionable and be derided for doing so. Speech is free only for those who have the correct ideas.

Different constituents bring different needs to the University of Michigan, its president reports. Students and parents want high-quality education and low costs; businesses seek useful graduates and research findings; patients at its hospital look for the best care; federal, state, and local governments help the university and regulate many of its activities.

Over the years, universities have been pressed to go beyond providing education, research, and service to offer health care, cultural centers, entertainment, on-the-job training, and social mobility. They have been urged to improve precollege education, ensure economic development, show how unlike cultures can live in peace, and help international understanding ("Multiple Roles Compel . . .", 1991). Boards for other organizations such as hospitals, libraries, associations, churches, fraternities, service clubs, welfare societies, social clubs, or communities of elders face comparable pressures.

Motivations of Advocates

Usually, people who are instructed by their board to put a new process in place do so. Less often, they question the board's request because they have a different view about what kind of change is needed. They recognize that they cannot change a board's decision by themselves because they are not equipped to do so, their board has the final say about a modifying a situation, or they need the support of others who have a similar preference. Therefore, they urge others to help them in their efforts. They appeal to the board and their supporters for any of four reasons.

First, they appeal to the board because the board is improperly ignoring problems that should be addressed. The advocates describe what they think a proper solution should be. Second, they hear that the board is considering a change on a particular problem, and they wish to influence its decision. Third, they object to a decision or policy of the board because it is causing tension, misunderstanding, or unhappiness among those living under it. Fourth, the advocates point to an opportunity that will benefit constituents but that is being overlooked by the board.

A few advocates seldom have enough power to convince executives or board members to make a change, so they join hands with other like-minded people on the assumption that the influence of a large group will be more potent than that of a small group. This group of activists then presses board members to move in a specific direction (Zander, 1985, 1990).

Boards of nonprofit organizations often hear conflicting views from different groups. A school board, for example, may be urged by different groups to move in contrasting directions on such issues as drugs, sports, sex education, content of textbooks, prayer in the classroom, or student haircuts (Bendiner, 1969). Demands by a state may be opposed by local citizens, which puts the school board in the middle. A school board cannot ignore its state's requirements but neither can it sweep aside the protests of parents. As Banfield and Wilson (1963) note, the board of an agency providing social welfare receives opposing pressures from haves versus have-nots, suburban residents versus downtown dwellers, one ethnic group versus another, whites versus blacks, conservatives versus liberals, nogrowth advocates versus property developers, and supporters of compassion at any price versus opponents of excessive spending.

Members of a board face pressure from dissimilar views among themselves; varied pressures from sources outside their group; strong forces from those who oppose their ideas; and conflicting questions, advice, or proposals from people who speak at their meetings. Problem solving and decision making can be com-

plex when contradictory ideas are pushed on the board and cannot
be ignored.

Responses to Advocates

When nonmembers bring a proposal before a board, board members
ignore the advocates, listen courteously, or actively welcome their
comments. Under special circumstances, they refuse to consider new
ideas or reject them outright. Which of these responses board
members choose depends to some degree on the style activists use
in presenting their plan.

Ignoring Advocates. When board members receive a request
from nonmembers to appear before the board, they may wish to
avoid these people's comments. They may write to the group or
individual, say no, and explain why they refuse. If an unwelcome
advocate takes the floor at an open meeting of the board, members
may avoid a confrontation by postponing consideration of the matter involved, perhaps hoping that the issue can later be tabled or
forgotten.

Sometimes a new suggestion is put aside because its sponsors
have incorrect assumptions about who decides what. University students or financial supporters of a school, for example, may ask
regents to tell faculty members what they should teach. These critics
do not realize that curricular decisions are made by the faculty
members and do not involve input from regents. Other reasons for
setting aside a request are that the advocates have few allies, weak
expertise in the matter at hand, no right to put pressure on the
board, or little ability to reward or threaten board members. Or they
may be seen by board members as troublemakers who can safely be
disregarded.

Members of a board evade a request if it is illogical, incomprehensible, or defies good sense. Poorly stated demands are often
based on anger or fear and contain little more than an expression
of such feelings. Or the requests may be contrary to the experience
of the board and seen as unworkable. A suggestion may be too costly
or too difficult to implement. Board members may be offended if a
proposed scheme is immoral, unethical, illegal, or breaks with
long-standing tradition. They try to pass over a plan that does not

fit the board's basic purposes or the charter of the organization they govern and pay minimal attention to a request that can set a bad precedent or helps few people but harms many. And they show little interest in a plan to fix matters that are, as they see things, not in need of repair.

If a group of protesters persists in applying pressure on a board, the board members might resort to reducing the power of the other group so it cannot be influential. They try to prevent the group from ever forming, or from continuing if it gets started. They solicit help from lawmakers and police in establishing curfews against advocates through antisubversion laws, strict barriers against libel, regulations to restrict the nature of bargaining, tight rules on demonstrating, prohibitions against parades, taxes on unwelcome activities, evictions from public places, restrictions against disturbing the peace, or narrow rules for gathering on company property. They justify such measures by contending that the advocates are a threat to law and order and that the community must protect itself against potential chaos.

Boards short-circuit the demands of other groups by coming up with a program that preempts the ideas of the advocates. For example, they propose a building program of their own, a plan for fostering community pride, or a way to develop a new program that makes the other group's ideas unnecessary. As a last resort, they take the matter to court, or appeal to a government agency that can intervene when asked for help. The procedures just described typically change the disagreement from one of substance to one of resistance over the style board members employ. In most instances, these procedures escalate the disagreement rather than resolve it.

Granting Advocates a Hearing. Members of a board hear a suggestion for change (without committing themselves) if the speakers address a problem that the board members know exists but have not resolved. For example, a school board may readily listen to ideas for financing educational activities, the directors of a professional society will listen to critics who say that their association will lose its tax-exempt status unless it stops making public pronouncements on political issues, and leaders of a church will listen to suggestions on raising funds for a new building.

Board members will grant a hearing to individuals who

bring an important issue before the board if the individuals stress the significance of this condition by describing the unfavorable consequences of ignoring it. For example, decision makers for a condominium will listen to individuals stating that fires will spread quickly if they start in the dry grass near its buildings and that wooden-shingle roofs on homes heighten this danger. University regents will listen to warnings that a majority of the faculty members are nearing the age of retirement, and younger blood is needed. A board of directors for a youth club will listen to critics stating that their programs are out-of-date because they no longer appeal to a generation educated by television.

Welcoming Suggestions. Several conditions foster the readiness of board members to go beyond mere listening and to welcome the advice or urgings of external agents. Members of a board being pressed by external agents to make a change deal with the advocates more comfortably if the advocates' goals and their own are similar. Where objectives are compatible, decision makers are more willing to hear an advocate's proposal and the advocate is more willing to cooperate with members of the board. Both the advocate and the board members realize they have similar aims, so they help one another accomplish what should be done (Deutsch, 1973; Zander, 1990).

Boards with less social power than those who urge them to make a change will be responsive to external pressures. For example, the board of a community park that is being urged by officials of the state government to allow oil drilling in the park, a parent-teacher association being told by the court that crosstown busing for school children must be established, or the board of a welfare rights organization being informed that controls on rental rates are being removed are likely to comply. Such boards and their constituents may protest these powerfully backed changes, but they will be lucky if they manage to modify the ideas of agents who have enough influence to ignore protests against their actions.

People who ask for consideration of their special views will be uneasy if the board they address is composed of superiors who determine the speakers' fate. In such an instance, board members should assure speakers that they will listen closely by promising not to oppose new ideas without hearing them in full and by assuring presenters that the goals of board members are similar to their own (where this is true). Such reassurance reduces fear, misunderstanding, or insecurity the speakers bring to a meeting with a board (Lebow and Stein, 1987).

Accountability to a Parent Organization

Organizations with similar goals often form an association that sets and enforces standards for their procedures and products. For example, an accrediting agency for universities and schools in a geographical area sends an evaluation committee to each of the member campuses in that association and looks into adequacy of books in the library, appropriateness of research facilities, number of full-time professors, the training of professors, kinds of subjects taught, and quality of courses. An accrediting association can demand that a school make specified improvements. If these changes are not put in place within a reasonable time, the offending school loses its accreditation. In that case, credits a student earns at the school will not be accepted by an accredited school, and high-caliber teachers will avoid teaching at the institution.

Other boards, for example, those of local congregations of a religious denomination or associations or societies that oversee local chapters, have limits put on them by a larger organization that fosters their existence. Governing boards of the smaller units are expected to abide by instructions from the parent organization.

Members of a board seldom avoid pressure from persons to whom they are directly accountable. In some instances, however, board members are not sure to whom they are accountable. For example, the members of a board of education know they should keep constituents informed and listen to parents' comments. But they may not realize that they are also beholden to the superintendent of schools and to the principals and teachers in their system because those people are educational professionals who need to understand and support the board's plans. Other groups, such as the parent-teacher association, budget setters and tax collectors of the city, the chamber of commerce, a ministers' association, and service clubs, do not have a right to insist on being told what the board is thinking and doing, but they may ask for information and for a chance to comment on the board's moves, which a board is usually prepared to provide.

Members of a board of regents for a private university may feel only limited obligations to faculty members and nearly none to students. More commonly, their eyes are on financial contributors, current and potential, from among alumni and friends. Regents for a public university commonly keep state legislators abreast of events on campus.

Legal Rules and Regulations

Laws and the rules of regulating agencies control activities of boards. These requirements are enforced by inspectors, examiners, or police. The regulations concern such areas as food handling, facilities for the handicapped, sexual abuse, safe transportation, control of asbestos, immunization, or restrictions on political activities. New rules regularly arise in respect to taxes; insurance; stewardship of pension funds; employment compensation; social security; or how individuals are to be treated, disciplined, taught, selected, judged, or given opportunities for jobs. Additional laws control access to and concealment of research information and its classification as secret. And a host of modern health-related regulations limit the treatment of people who are subjects in research, the use of animals in medical investigations, work with recombinant DNA, studies of viruses, storage of carcinogens and radioactive material, and disposal of waste.

In the past, all laws dealt with the behavior of individuals but not with that of social bodies or corporations because the latter were considered to be legal fictions "with no pants to kick or soul to damn" (Stone, 1975, p. 6). Illegal actions could not be attributed to an organization, only to an individual, and therefore a group could never break a law. A member of a corporation could not be held responsible for actions made in behalf of the corporation because his or her liability was limited to specific things he or she had been told to do by a superior—and no one was ever told, of course, to break the law. By 1860, according to Stone, corporations were no longer ignored as wrongdoers.

Today, all kinds of laws limit the actions of all kinds of organizations, nonprofit or profit. Groups who are given taxpayers' money or provide a service for clients are watched by government to be sure they give what they promise.

For example, a state legislative body grants the right to a community to create a school board for its area. A state's department of education imposes rules regulating required courses, who may teach, or what books may be used. It also enforces requirements concerning transportation of pupils, care of their health, insurance, or civil service. Because a state provides much of the income for a community's schools, it can say, "Do as we order, or your subsidy will be reduced" (Reeves, 1954; Goldhammer, 1964).

David Funk (1982) examined the effects of government's rules upon organizations and coined the term *group dynamic law* in describing these restraints. According to Funk, group dynamic laws are the ones that have a strong impact on the cohesion and integration of groups who work under them. Often, these laws have harmful effects. Funk urges lawmakers to recognize that regulations can damage an organization they constrain.

The way a law is written and made known has a great deal to do with whether boards and their constituents abide by it. Groups are more likely to accept a regulation if the need for the rule was originally suggested by those it is to govern or if the wording of the rule was influenced by those people it regulates. Compliance is more widespread and smoother if drafts of a bill are made available for comments by those to be controlled by it. The size of a fine that a guilty body will have to pay, the length of a jail sentence for convicted officials, and the threatened loss of a license or other privileges are also likely to stimulate obedient attention. But persons who participate in the development of a regulation probably feel more favorably about the rule (leading to positive acceptance) than do those who have a new regulation forced upon them and who must obey that law in order to avoid punishments. The fairness of a law, in the eyes of those it controls, has perhaps as much effect on its acceptability as its content or requirements.

A general statement describing the essence of obedience goes like this: the strength of compliance to a new regulation depends on the amount of compatibility between its content and current practices in the organization as well as the value members place on what the rule requires. Members of a board and those they govern are more likely to comply with a rule when they believe it promises a better way to achieve important ends than previously had been the case.

When board and staff members discuss how they will implement a rule, they consider to whom the law applies, what those persons must change, how they can be helped to make those changes, and how the degree of adherence can be monitored. Members of a board are ultimately responsible for the acts of the employees of their organization, so they need to know whether workers are in fact obeying relevant laws.

Most board members are drawn from a pool of leaders whose actions are visible to observers, the press, or peers; they are prominent individuals. These individuals ordinarily obey regulations faithfully because they are good citizens and expect such behavior from one another. Board members will work against a rule or drag their feet in complying with it if obedience to it will generate unpleasant consequences for the organization they govern, the new rule is not needed, or the results of complying with it will be less satisfactory than practices currently followed.

The way a rule is presented to targeted groups or the way adherence to it is demanded will arouse the opposition of these groups if regulation is seen to be capricious, arbitrary, amateurish, or ill advised. Also, board members may avoid a regulation if it is petty in detail, technically inaccurate, incomprehensible, inconsistent within itself, or constantly revised. They do not happily accept a rule if it demands unnecessary work in completing forms, obtaining data, training staff members, revising equipment, or keeping records. They may object if a rule is not enforced or if it cannot be enforced because transgressions of it are not detectable. They may not respect a rule if sanctions put on those who break it are too weak to worry about or too small to do any harm.

Board members may justify opposition to a new regulation by claiming that their charter limits their freedom to change, their group's basic purpose forbids certain modifications, or a superior organization places strict boundaries on their actions. They may also indicate what qualities they can or cannot modify without others' approval. If they decide to reject the rule, they give reasons for their refusal in a way that generates minimal resistance among agents supporting the change.

Summary

The board of a nonprofit agency operates within external constraints and outside pressures. Active social pressures on a board arise from groups of constituents who wish to benefit themselves or their supporters by influencing the board to make particular moves. These advocates appeal to the board because they want it to act on a problem it has ignored, want to influence the board's decision on an issue it is facing, object to past actions by the board, or want to point to an opportunity the board should seize.

Because they occupy publicly prominent positions, board members are obliged to respond when agents of influence urge them to listen. Their reactions may try to ignore the activists, grant the activists a hearing, or openly welcome suggestions.

Boards obey demands made of them by a larger organization of which they are a part and to which they are accountable. Ordinarily, they abide by requirements of lawmakers or regulatory agencies, unless these demands are unwise, too burdensome, or press for too great a transformation.

6

Powers of Influence

Increasing the Board's Ability
to Implement Decisions

Members of a board influence nonmembers when their actions change the behavior or beliefs of the individuals. People who cause such a change are said to have social power over those they influence. Several features of the origin and use of social power are worth discussing here. This discussion is based on writings by the following scholars: Cartwright (1965), French and Raven (1959), Kipnis (1976), Zander (1990), and Raven (1992).

Board members who have power in their relations with others are ordinarily able to influence certain groups and individuals only in specific matters. For example, a board of education may convince a city council to act on a problem concerning after-school recreation programs or library hours but not on other issues such as parking structures or activities of the health department. Moreover, a board of education may affect the views of members of the parent-teacher association but have no influence with people in the chamber of commerce or American Legion. The directors of a community center can require that all programs be held in the center's building but will not have much impact on ways of teaching music there or how the basketball team is coached.

Board members who know they can influence certain people on specific issues may choose not to display their power. Instead, they keep it in abeyance until they wish to use it. Thus, board members may not reveal their power often or at all. They may have the right and authority to set policies, fire the chief executive, develop new regulations, or ignore constituents, but they may seldom do those things.

Members of some boards do not realize the power they have over certain groups and individuals. For example, people may admire the board members but not reveal these feelings. They may try to behave like board members do because they view board members as models. Or when listeners believe board members are experts, they may adopt the trustees' views without revealing their feelings of respect for the trustees. Thus board members can be influential without overtly trying to be.

Some kinds of power come to board members or are granted to them because they know a lot about a matter, even if they do not press their ideas when this topic comes up for discussion. The power of experts derives from the readiness of others to perceive them as wise men or women and to ask them for information or advice. An expert has no power, however, if no one sees him or her as an expert, no one knows that the individual spent years studying and working on the matter at hand, or no one asks the well-informed person for help in his or her area of expertise. In such a case, the expert is unheralded, ignored, and powerless.

Social power is a two-way proposition. In a two-sided discussion, each party commonly influences the other to some degree. Advocates of a given change may influence listeners in certain respects and have their own views modified while doing so. This process of informing while being informed occurs in negotiating, bargaining, and problem solving.

Why do board members press nonmembers to change? First, they fear that the mere announcement of a decision will not carry enough weight among those who are expected to adopt the change. Second, targeted groups and individuals may question the decisions of board members to protect themselves from being influenced.

As noted in Chapter Four, board members often help nonmembers recognize the value of a change they propose so that these constituents will be at ease with the new plan. Some board decisions are unpopular, even opposed. If members believe the changes must be implemented and enforced without fail, despite opposition to them, they try to overcome others' reluctance by showing them how they will benefit if they go along with the proposal or will be penalized if they do not. In such a case, board members do not point to internal satisfactions a listener will derive from the change but offer rewards or penalties as incentives to make the change.

How Board Members Try to Influence Nonmembers

Members of a board choose among several methods to get their way when targeted individuals question their plans. These procedures range from persuading to coercing.

Persuasion

Persuasion is a planned effort to control the beliefs or behaviors of particular individuals. People using persuasion deliver information, but the content of their comments is intentionally one sided and urgent. They want to convince listeners that no views or actions other than ones being advocated are sensible. Moreover, they do not wish to consider contrary claims. They try to restrict alternatives available to those in their audience by telling them that if the listeners continue their present course or choose a different way from the one the speaker is putting forth, the listeners will be making a mistake.

Persuasion is a way of mildly warning listeners about the unfavorable consequences of incorrect behavior, a means for showing people a better path, or both. Persuasion arouses a desire among those addressed to avoid unwanted side effects or to achieve gains from behaving as they are being urged to do. Board members who use persuasion believe they know the best course of action, so they sell their point of view strongly.

Persuasion depends on information that is inherently compelling and on data and derivations from such data. Board members who are trying to persuade nonmembers call on other board members and experts who can support their case. They avoid getting into a debate because ordinary give-and-take may force them to recognize counterarguments. They do not engage in problem solving or seek the soundest solution because they want their ideas to be embraced and implemented soon.

People who are trying to persuade others use special rhetorical devices so their ideas will prevail over the views of listeners. Deutsch (1973) suggests several parts of a strategy for effective persuasion. First, the speaker should make the proposal clear to those addressed, so that the latter will know what is expected of them. Clarity eliminates opposition due to misunderstanding of the request. Second, the speaker should state in sympathetic terms that members of the audience will probably have problems in accepting the ideas being offered and that the speaker will help the listeners and others overcome these difficulties. Third, how the listeners will benefit if they do what is being proposed must be demonstrated, and as many gains as possible should be cited. Fourth, the speaker should point out that others in the organization or community will benefit from the change. Fifth, the speaker should state flatly that the intention is to make the targeted individuals change and that the speaker will advise them on how to implement the improvements being pushed. Sixth, how everyone's objectives will be compromised if these changes are not made should be pointed out.

Even though members of a board believe a change they desire is important, they ordinarily depend on factual information, reason, and authority to win their way, not on excessive debate. They are unlikely to use emotional behavior such as hostility, pleas, or phony friendliness in supporting their cause because board members seldom get into situations where they have to push their preferences hard. That task usually falls to executive officers. Sometimes, however, a board must defend an action it has taken or contemplates taking. In such cases, board members may believe that the end is important, so the means do not matter. They may turn to propaganda and abandon dependence on facts.

Propaganda

When persuasion is wholly couched in emotion-laden terms, it is called *propaganda*. The individuals using propaganda appeal to their listeners' emotions, pleasant or unpleasant, by shading the truth, exaggerating the unfavorableness of conditions, or arousing fears or greed. According to Thum and Thum (1972), propagandists depend on devices like the following:

- Generating fears of what could happen if a change is not made
- Appealing to listeners' desires to be more fashionable, influential, higher in status, and so on
- Distracting listeners by emphasizing one thing in order to hide another (for example, sidetracking criticism by accusing critics of being disloyal or by stressing that a topic that is not pertinent to the issue at hand)
- Using distorted logic while emphasizing the rationality of the statements being made ("Everyone knows that . . .")
- Presenting complicated problems in terms of slogans or stereotypes and thereby oversimplifying issues
- Using loaded words to describe the opposition (lazy, greedy, stingy, unpatriotic, parolees)
- Deceiving by use of falsehoods as facts

People who use propaganda press their views by making sure that only a small part of a controversial question gets a full hearing. Their demands "are peremptory. . . . [They] assert truths that they present as inescapable, defying argument, so essentially true that they are beyond the need for corroborating evidence" (Bailey, 1983, p. 125). They recognize that their arguments are biased but defend their style by saying they are supporting what is right or have chosen to make an emotional appeal because a factual method does not loosen listeners' hold on their mistaken beliefs.

Bailey (1983) says that one cannot sensibly ask whether an argument advanced by a propagandist is valid or invalid, nor can one test it by the rules of logic. One can only ask whether it is effective because it changed the views of targeted individuals. Rationality (persuasion) requires training to use well, but anyone can effectively use passion (propaganda). Bailey says that passion is stronger than rationality because listeners to an emotional presentation defend their views in passionate terms, and doing so makes them immune to rational arguments. Rational arguments have a weaker impact on listeners than passionate ones because they cause people to doubt, penetrate, and criticize rather than yield.

Certain styles of speaking, according to Bailey, make propaganda more effective than persuasion. These include describing oneself as a moral person who has worked hard for the good of the organization; demonstrating one's useful ties with members of the audience; showing that one speaks with authority because of experience and the sound values underlying the change one is advancing; citing warnings of future events that must not be ignored; recalling the threat inherent in the proposals made by objecting persons; focusing on the feelings of listeners, not on their deeds; and praising or condemning people, not their actions.

Bargaining

If persuasion or propaganda do not work or seem improper, board members may turn to bargaining in the hope that they will gain some things by giving up others. They intend to agree to a bargain to gain more than they offer. But to do so, they must have enough power to influence the acts of targeted individuals and yet not be seen as pleaders who seek a compromise because they are weak. They may believe they have such power because they are members of an official and legitimate body and have convinced targeted individuals to engage in bargaining. They recognize, moreover, that they have control over things that people on the other side covet, such as promotions, higher wages, publicity, longer vacations, better working conditions, or training to improve skills. Board members also sense that their ideas can be improved during the discussions inherent in bargaining and that the people on the other side may become so involved in the board's proposal that they do not demand much in the deliberations.

After a bargaining session, if one side gains more than the other, the winners feel satisfied with themselves and are at ease, but losers examine, evaluate, and improve on their previous argument so they can bargain better in the future. In the long run, losers may benefit more than winners from the bargaining process because they try to improve their future strategy while winners are content with their victory.

Bargaining is most useful when both sides are fairly equal in their ability to influence; otherwise, those with greater power (usually board members) will be inclined to listen little, talk a lot, and push plans in directions that suit themselves. Effective two-way bargaining requires that members on one side offer to compromise—to give in on an issue or two—expecting that those on the other side will do likewise. If a compromise is not offered by one side or the other, the bargaining becomes stalled and little progress can be made.

An initial compromise usually involves something that is not too precious and that the proposers know the other side wants. A response to such an offer likewise involves something desirable to the opposing side. Ideally, the sacrifice and satisfaction should be equal for people on both sides.

In bargaining, there is a danger in making the first proposal because opponents may see this as a sign of weakness. Thus, the individuals who accept the initial offer may not make a counteroffer because they now see themselves as being in a superior position. Therefore, a bargaining session is more fruitful if both parties have a fair understanding of what the other party wants and are able to satisfy that desire during bargaining. Neither side should offer anything that is considerably more valuable than what the other can give, since doing so makes the offer appear to be a bribe.

If board members approach bargaining as a contest they badly want to win, they use special tactics. To be sure they will come out ahead, they must gain more and give up less than the other individuals involved. Accordingly, they try to learn the preferences of the people with whom they are bargaining, know what the others can offer, make a counteroffer, and emphasize that this is the last chance for a settlement. The board will give no more. Truly competitive bargainers set their initial stakes high so that rivals will feel compelled to bargain for fear of the consequences if they do not. Demands stated in strong terms may lead people on the other side to recognize that they cannot get all they want from such hard bargainers and to keep their own requests low.

If people in one party intend to benefit as a result of bargaining, they cannot let themselves give in to threats, pressures, or other forms of coercion. They also cannot let differences between themselves and the other side escalate in such a way that people on either side will not listen and conflict replaces bargaining. Conflict generates resistance to bargaining.

Rewards

Board members, compared to most of their constituents, are better able to promise rewards and deliver them. These rewards include a picture in the newspaper, a raise in pay, new facilities, medals, a banquet in the targeted group's honor, or a day of celebration for the group. Targeted groups reject such rewards, however, if they see these as bribes, payoffs, inadequate prizes, or illegitimate nudgings.

Reasons for the use of rewards are well known. People who offer a reward believe it will arouse the interest of individuals who otherwise might be complacent about a proposed change because the change itself does not promise satisfaction. A reward may indicate approval for past behavior, and its recipients are led to understand they will be blessed again if they repeat their good actions. A reward that is given in public shows onlookers that good actions are rewarded and that anyone else who behaves in the same fashion will also be rewarded.

Experience and research show that a person who gets a reward is grateful toward those who provide it but not if the reward is seen to be payment for services agreed upon and rendered. A reward also is not an effective incentive if it is not valued by the receiver. If the same reward is offered repeatedly, moreover, its value falls, and it is no longer a source of satisfaction or a stimulant to action. Those who are rewarded over and over eventually raise their expectations and want more for the same amount of service.

People who do what they are told to do solely because of an offered reward are motivated to earn that reward, not to take steps they see as valuable or satisfying. The reward, not the change, is the incentive. When this is the case, people often do only as much, and no more, than is necessary to earn the reward. They make their actions visible to the people who want the change so that these people know the actions deserve to be rewarded. Board members watch potential rewardees to be sure they do the things that warrant reward.

Because the overt actions of targeted individuals can be observed, rewards are a useful way to encourage innovations in behavior and to make sure these occur. However, it is difficult to determine if the individuals have changed their beliefs and attitudes. They may say they have revised their beliefs when they have not changed them at all.

Coercion

In some instances, board members forcefully demand changes in the behavior of those they wish to influence. They do not intend to allow a choice in the matter, so they threaten to punish the targeted individuals if these people do not comply with the board's demands. In threatening to use punishment, board members are engaging in *coercion*.

A coercive act places limits on the freedom of choice of the people to whom it is directed. The threatened penalty is deliberately repulsive, and to avoid this punishment, people being coerced usually do what is asked of them. The more undesirable the punishment, the stronger the coercion. If the targeted individuals see the penalty as mild or unlikely to occur, they will pay little attention to coercive demands.

Like the use of rewards, the use of coercion changes overt behavior more readily than covert beliefs since visible actions can easily be monitored but ideas and attitudes cannot. Therefore, people who use coercion usually spy on the individuals they put under pressure or hire informers to make sure a punishment will be delivered when deserved. The threat of coercion, its actual use, and the subsequent surveillance of people who are being pressed to change generate poor interpersonal relations between the agents of change and the targeted group. The troubled relationship then becomes a separate problem to be resolved.

Members of a board might use coercion for several reasons. Trustees become angry if the response of those they govern is derogatory or hostile. Such a response usually implies that the board members' use of more permissive methods has failed. If nothing else works, the board members may believe that force must be employed. The targeted individuals may flatly refuse to do what they are asked. So board members may say the refusal justifies their use of penalties and threats. Board members may feel confident that this approach will be successful because it has been in the past (Kipnis, 1976; Zander, 1990).

Nonmember activists who wish to exert coercive pressure on a board may use aggressive procedures. In one approach, they keep board members from doing their regular work through a sit-in, a noisy sabotage of a meeting, a boycott, or a hostile demonstration. In a second approach, they physically limit the freedom of board members, seize one or more of the members, and keep board members under guard while declaring these prisoners will not be freed until the activists' requirements are met. Or they lock board members in their meeting room until the members yield to their demands. In a third approach, they damage property, hurt board members, or threaten such harm if their demands are not met. Coercive acts call the public's attention to the actors' grievances and serve to overcome the inertia of listeners, forcing them to attend to issues they have been avoiding (Zander, 1990).

Board members may use a few aggressive methods of coercion, such as locking out dissidents, arresting or suing leaders of opposing groups, or harming the reputations of troublemakers. They seldom initiate physically aggressive procedures because these interfere with the operation of the organization and make it difficult for the board to work effectively. When members of a board are faced with hostile behavior, their immediate impulse is to counter such actions with similar ones. Aggressive emotions then increase on both sides as the nonmembers feel impelled to escalate their aggressive behavior. The conflict may be limited if leaders on both sides recognize that calmer forms of interaction are needed and that hostility will waste everyone's time.

Most board members are more motivated to help the people they govern than to satisfy personal wishes. Thus, they seldom use coercion. Critics of a board, by contrast, mostly seek to get gains for themselves or their group by urging board members to take certain actions. If they do not win what they seek, they feel free to coerce the board in whatever way they can. They have little interest in the fate of the board or in those the board governs.

Effects of Serving on a Powerful Board

In fifty-three of California's fifty-eight counties, the superintendent of schools has more power than the locally elected trustees who hire him or her. The state's education code grants this power. The superintendent usually asks the board to ratify his or her actions, however, and board members respond while being aware that the superintendent can successfully insist on having his or her own way (Ezekiel, 1991). Such legally established power of a CEO over his or her governing board is rare in other kinds of nonprofit organizations.

When, in contrast, board members have power over the CEO and staff, they derive several benefits. They readily achieve prized personal goals while serving on the board because they can make things happen as they desire and few others can block these moves. In serving their own needs, moreover, they can get the help of the executives and employees they govern. They are usually treated deferentially by subordinates and are often approved of, complimented, or offered privileges by subordinates. Not surprisingly, members are more attracted to a board that has greater power. They come to see their power as a valued end in itself and as a natural part of their role as a board member. They develop an attachment to power, do not want to lose it, and try to preserve it (Zander, Cohen, and Stotland, 1957; Cartwright and Zander, 1968; Kipnis, 1976; Zander, 1982).

Because they have more power than their subordinates, board members are more comfortable with subordinates than vice versa. It is not uncommon for decision makers to use their power in ways that deprive others but reward themselves. They may allot excessive rewards (such as compensation for attending conventions, travel expenses, and insurance) to their group and justify such expenditures as deserved by persons of their status but not by others.

Subordinates may be unsure of how to act toward superiors if the latter seldom use their influence during board meetings and are passive or unassertive while staff members do most of the talking. How should constituents deal with such members of a board? What should they expect of them? How will these board members reveal their power? Individuals governed by a board resolve such uncertainties by trying to win the goodwill of the trustees. They tolerate demeaning behavior by board members that they would not accept from other people. They tell board members that they agree with them and approve of their actions when they do not.

Board members, in light of such deferential acts, tend to believe that their ideas are sound because they get little feedback that would tell them otherwise. Thus, the possession of power and others' reactions to it often cause board members to develop exalted views of their competence and make them feel they know far more than the people they govern (which may not be the case). Accordingly, a board member may have little respect for the ability of subordinates unless those individuals help the board in very effective ways.

Not all people with power develop inflated egos, of course. Most board members use their power gently while monitoring the organization they guide. Their actions can be helpful to others because they have the freedom and power to implement their more kindly dispositions. People who are sure of their influence have more self-confidence, are ordinarily less defensive, and tend to be more supportive in relations with subordinates than people who are unsure of their power. A powerful board, according to Kipnis (1976), will help others more often than hinder them, except when others challenge the board or try to reduce its power.

Board's Power Versus Chief Executive's Power

If boards have strong methods available for exerting social power, why is their behavior often seen as too passive? Perhaps boards are seen as passive because they exercise their influence poorly. Board members need skill, prior planning, and organized effort, to persuade, propagandize, bargain, reward, or coerce. The same is true of the methods for informing nonmembers of decisions and involving nonmembers in decision making, described in Chapter Four. Aside from members' poor skills or unattractive styles of trying to influence others, certain situations in a board's surroundings may weaken its power.

Bendiner (1969, p. 31) states that "responsibility flows to the nearest paid authority." Therefore, members of boards tend to encourage their organization's CEO to plan, take actions, and evaluate outcomes—to make moves, in short, that could (or should) be decided by the board. An executive who is asked to do these things, especially one who thinks of himself or herself as a trained professional, is happy to guide the actions of (the amateur) board members. Some nonprofit organizations governed by boards, such as social agencies, schools, libraries, or churches, are frequently exposed to new fads in their operations and services. Board members may call on their chief official to help them appraise these new ideas. According to Zeigler, Kehoe, and Reisman (1985), board members grant some of their power to management so they can make a wiser decision.

Boards for business firms often tend to look to the CEO of the company, not the president of the board, as their leader. Lorsch and MacIver (1989) asked directors of commercial corporations how much influence the chief executive had in their board's decisions. Of the respondents, 44 percent said "a great deal" and 55 percent said "very much." When asked why the CEO was so powerful, they said that the CEO knew more than the board did about company affairs, prepared the agenda of meetings, decided what information should be given the board, and chose most of the board members, and that his or her ideas carried extra weight in board meetings.

Lorsch and MacIver also asked directors about their personal participation in board meetings. Fifty percent of the respondents said they felt no constraints on contributing and talked whenever they were so inclined. The rest typically did not speak in meetings because board meetings were hurried, they had no expertise in topics being discussed, they lacked information on the issue at hand, or they had little time to prepare for a session. A majority, 83 percent, said that the dominance of the CEO did not keep them from talking, nor did they think that the CEO abused his or her power during sessions of the board. Forty-nine percent said they never spoke in board meetings for fear they would look foolish. How often, one wonders, do board members for nonprofit organizations refrain from speaking because of these factors?

Mace (1986) studied nearly two hundred board members of corporations and found that the CEO of a company usually is granted the greatest control of meetings because board members lack necessary knowledge about events in the company. The top executive thus determines, in large part, what the directors discuss, decide, and do. Mace believes most business managers are aware that their power is greater than the power of the board members and try to use it in a way that is acceptable to the board. The CEO tells the board members that their help is useful to him or her but makes sure the board provides only advice and counsel, not binding decisions. Chief executives say they are willing to be moderate during meetings because they know they can have their own way if they must. Are boards of nonprofit organizations different?

I know head officers of nonprofit organizations who keep specific issues off the agenda at board meetings because these matters are too complicated for members to understand and a resolution of the issues by board members would be ill informed. Such clipping of the agenda is probably more likely to occur in an organization that deals with abstruse matters like the planning of research programs, therapy, or religious doctrines. Even though board members have their power reduced in this way, they probably do not mind because people dislike making decisions on matters they do not understand. They fear they may make a poor choice and not realize they have done so.

Members of a board can create conditions that earn them greater influence. They may hire an executive officer to run the organization and thus relieve themselves of concern over administrative details and devote their energy and wisdom to establishing policies and planning to meet long-term issues. They must keep in mind, however, that the chief executive is accountable to them—he or she is the only employee board members supervise. All other employees work for this head officer, who is responsible for the quality of their output. Trustees should inform the CEO, in precise terms, what the board expects him or her to accomplish in the next year or so. They also should state limitations on the executive's freedom of action and periodically evaluate that person's performance. A board can have power over its executive if it defines the relationship between trustees and the executive as one in which members of the board are in charge (Carver, 1990).

Lorsch and MacIver (1989) name several sources of power for members of a company's board. These include the legal authority granted to those serving on a board, sufficient confidence to express their own views, knowledge and information about the topic under discussion, unity among board members, and control over setting the agenda. But members of a board are seldom blamed for unpopular changes within an organization, which is a sign to Lorsch and MacIver that observers do not believe that trustees are responsible for innovations. Perhaps board members should make their responsibility for decisions known. Doing so will expose them to derogation or credit, as the case may be. It will also earn them a reputation as doers and people of influence.

Summary

A governing board has power over others when its actions change the beliefs or behaviors of those individuals. When board members require that their decision be implemented by targeted individuals who are not eager to comply, they use any of several methods: persuasion, propaganda, bargaining, rewards, or coercion. People being pushed to accept a board's mandate in these ways pay less attention to the quality or satisfactoriness of plans proposed by the board than to the incentives the board offers (correct information, a bargain, a reward, or avoidance of a penalty or punishment).

Because members of a board are in a position to determine the fate of subordinates and stakeholders, these people tend to treat trustees in ways that make them self-centered, excessively confident of their superior wisdom, and protective of their status. Despite the likelihood that board members may have power to influence selected others, they may be ineffective in their efforts to influence the chief executive or staff of the organization they oversee, either because these paid personnel know more about the issues at hand or because the charter of the board gives more power to the professionals.

7

Groups in Conflict
Understanding Productive and Unproductive Outcomes

A conflict develops when two parties disagree about what each should or should not do. For example, the trustees of a housing community propose to build a new gatehouse, but protesters say the plan is too costly; the trustees of a religious body ask the city's planning commission to approve plans for construction of apartments for the elderly, entailing the removal of one hundred trees, but a group of arbor lovers urge the church to withdraw this request; the board of a hospital decides to close its unit for emergency care, but a nurses association opposes this action. Each of these disputes can become heated if neither side will compromise.

According to Zeigler, Kehoe, and Reisman (1985), a conflict arises when one side tries to block the other side's achievement of a goal. These authors are interested in the kinds of disputes that occur when an action by an elected school board or city council is opposed by a group of critics and a basic interest of one party is assailed by the other. The authors report that city councils get into more conflicts than school boards and that a council's disagreements are more severe and more concerned with basic policy. Members of school boards disagree with one another more often than do members of city councils.

A given action by one group generates a conflict if it prevents, obstructs, interferes, injures, or in some way makes another group less effective. For example, students at a college will not

117

allow the regents to hold a meeting unless they are promised that more minority individuals will be hired as professors. A minister of a church refuses to meet with his board because members make such poor decisions. Parents protest when the school board abolishes team sports.

A conflict is wasteful if the tension it generates prevents participants from thinking clearly or making sound decisions. A conflict is useful if it awakens interest and curiosity that lead to the airing of problems that are being ignored and to efforts toward improving things. This chapter examines the origins of disputes, what causes them to become wasteful, and their effects.

Origins of Conflicts Between
Boards and Other Groups

A conflict can develop because there is a short supply of desirable resources, such as funds, authority, privileges, or benefits (Deutsch, 1973). In such an instance, if members in one group are satisfied, those in the other cannot be. A school board, for example, desires a piece of land for a new educational center, and the fire department wants the same land. The computer center at a university requires more funds, but so does the library. The coaches of athletic teams at a university want a new stadium, but regents give priority to a new administration building.

Another cause of conflict is a strong emotional response, or resistance by decision makers to a style used by advocates as they present their ideas. The listeners resent the presenters' abrasive, discourteous, uncivil, or hostile manner, yet they respond with similar behavior. Angry emotions thereafter increase on both sides. Decision makers may be repelled as well if they believe those pushing a particular plan want only to benefit themselves or if the information they employ is not trustworthy. A conflict may also ensue, according to Deutsch (1973), if the tastes of one party impinge on the preferences of another; there is disagreement over what is true and what is false; both sides want to be dominant; or one side wants to collaborate with the other, but that offer is spurned.

Certain circumstances in the relationship between a board

and nonmembers can increase the likelihood of conflict. Some of the circumstances are discussed in the following sections.

Unclear Roles for Board Members and Nonmembers

Members of a board and their opposers have more conflicts if neither side understands clearly who is responsible for performing relevant tasks. For example, the division of labor between members of a school board and their superintendent is often hard to maintain. On some issues, such as deciding on details of the budget, the superintendent has the most say. In other instances, such as in calming complaining parents, the board has the most input. Bendiner (1969) states that school board members turn to the superintendent for advice on technical and professional matters but keep their own counsel on political issues. The board and superintendent may try to avoid onerous duties or claim jurisdiction over matters beneficial to themselves. In such cases, each party may feel the other is shirking its duties or seizing prerogatives that do not belong to it. Confusion encourages conflicts.

Lack of Settled Procedures for Resolving Conflicts

Tension is more likely to arise between groups if participants have little experience in settling strained relations or do not have set methods for resolving disputes. It takes skill to prevent friction from flowering into animosity. For example, if board members for a school system get into a disagreement with parents and the superintendent has been taught that conflict must be prevented at all costs because it damages the harmony that should always exist between the board and the community, board members will get no help from the superintendent. They will have to resolve the dispute themselves, despite lack of practice in resolving disputes (Zeigler, Kehoe, and Reisman, 1985).

When a university's board of regents must deal with a technical issue, for example, whether to allow research on recombinant DNA, board members may be unsure what to decide if separate sets of experts press them in opposing directions and if there is no clear evidence about what might happen if such research is allowed. Who should settle this kind of issue; the faculty of the medical school, all professors on the campus, the city council, local and distant voters, invited experts, or the regents alone (Zander, 1979)?

Disadvantaged Group Members

Conflicts are likely to develop if one group sees itself at a disadvantage compared to peers. For example, employees of a large social service agency may be dismayed if, compared to employees in similar agencies, they receive less pay for their work and have poorer working conditions, older equipment, or more burdensome tasks. If members of their board do not agree that the workers are disadvantaged, tension may develop between the workers and the trustees. Members of a governing board, for their part, seldom believe they are deprived in relations with employees because they usually have the power (if they use it) to make things happen as they like.

Conflict as an Enjoyable Contest

Conflicts develop more easily if participants in either party welcome a dispute. Banfield and Wilson (1963) say that politicians often see a disagreement as a game of matching wits that they enjoy for its own sake. Therefore, they like to keep the contest going. A variation on this notion happens among groups that wish to make powerful people unhappy. Groups of students glow over their skill in stalling meetings of regents. And members of boards hear from groups that bring up a different complaint regularly, some more frivolous than serious.

Loss of Respect for the CEO

If the board loses respect for its CEO, conflict is likely to develop. For example, the board of a church asked the minister to leave, and he refused. The board then asked members of the congregation to vote on whether the minister should stay or leave. Only 30 percent of the congregation's members wanted him to resign, but that was enough for the pastor. He resigned because he thought conflict was too probable.

Clearly, a chief executive will have more quarrels with his or her board if board members believe he or she is performing poorly. These difficulties will be exacerbated if separate members privately disapprove of the CEO but do not tell one another their opinions. The result is a "pluralistic ignorance," in which each member thinks the CEO is inept but does not realize that others think the same thing. Boards prevent such covert disapproval by regularly appraising their CEO's performance.

Board Faces a Crisis

Many boards accept their head officer's moves until a crisis occurs, such as a threat of financial loss or cancellation of the agency's license to operate. During a crisis, board members, managers, staff, and citizen observers may come into conflict over what to do.

Lorsch and MacIver (1989) studied crises in business boards. They say that courtesy usually prevails during these bad times: "The norms of delicate behavior and undiscussability [of conflicted issues] carry over when a board struggles with a crisis" (p. 164). But, they add, polite behavior often delays a resolution of a crisis because it prevents discussion of certain issues, and board members therefore never get to the bottom of things. These authors suggest that it may be necessary at times to deviate from the norms of courteous behavior to settle a conflict. Nonprofit boards probably respond in similar ways.

Factors That Heighten a Conflict

Certain factors make a dispute more intense and harder to control. These include polarization, escalation, internal social pressures toward uniformity, importance of the issue, cultural requirements, and social class of board members.

Polarization

If people on each side of a conflict are convinced that their ideas are wholly correct and the rivals' ideas are totally wrong, they are *polarized*—frozen in a state of disagreement. They argue in favor of their own beliefs and do not consider or even listen to others' suggestions. As a result, progress toward resolving the dispute will be slowed. People on each side release their grip on previous opinions only if they start speaking in terms that employ the views of opponents or try to learn what unstated needs those in the other party hope to settle by getting their way (Fisher, Ury, and Patton, 1991).

Escalation

As noted earlier, members of a board often respond to conflict by using the behavioral style of people who are trying to influence them. If nonmembers use an aggressive manner, board members may reply in a similar manner and arouse more aggression from the nonmembers. A destructive form of escalation can follow in which each side employs increasingly heated language and mannerisms.

A conflict is likely to escalate under any of three circumstances. First, participants on each side decide that those in the other party intend to satisfy their own interests, regardless of what happens to anyone else. This belief encourages those in the opposing groups to use cunning, trickery, or force in dealing with adversaries and to abandon fair play or courtesy in their determination to win.

Second, members of each group see their own motives as more appropriate, proper, and wise than those of the other group. The rivals' notions are viewed as wrong and evil. Rational analysis is abandoned for fear it will be taken as a sign of weakness. Third, participants excuse whatever inappropriate or harmful deeds they commit on the grounds that these are justified under the circumstances.

Internal Social Pressures Toward Uniformity

Members of a board who agree on their group's goals and on ways of attaining the goals put pressures on one another to abide by the group's decisions. When these pressures are strong, members think alike and hold firmly to their uniform views. They seldom accept ideas that are not like those of their group because they value membership in the group and fear they will be disapproved of by associates if they express unapproved views. As noted earlier, when a board is cohesive, members' strong desire to remain on the board makes members prone to adhere closely to their group's standards (Cartwright and Zander, 1968). Where conformity among board members is great, members are less willing to change their ideas or allow the other side to win. Strong support for a group's standards makes members rigid about their beliefs, which heightens any conflict over those topics.

Importance of Issue

A conflict becomes keener when the problem under contention is important to both sides. Board members do not take a dispute seriously if it concerns a matter that has no consequence for them or the organization they govern. What starts as a minor conflict may spread to include significant matters, and the intensity of a conflict can heighten. Conflicts grow in size and severity if allowed to do so.

Cultural Requirements

The severity of a quarrel between members of a board and nonmembers may become greater if they live in a culture that admires displays of anger or stubbornness. In some Latin American and Middle Eastern countries, for example, it is considered manly to take offense easily and respond aggressively to small affronts. In such places, those involved in a quarrel are urged on by supporters to defend their honor and are disapproved of if they do not. This culturally sanctioned aggression also occurs in some ethnic groups in the United States.

Brill (1971) tells how leaders of a rent strike at a city-owned housing project tried to frighten officials into meeting the strikers' demands. They used rehearsed behavior to show that they were angry and powerful. They stared stonily at the mayor while refusing to answer his questions (silent stubbornness was perceived to be a way of displaying strength), exaggerated the number of people taking part in the strike, used military terms when addressing one another in a public meeting, boasted publicly about the effectiveness of their hostile acts, and wore African tribal costumes to bargaining sessions.

Social Class of Board Members

Years ago, students of behavior observed that individuals from lower socioeconomic levels in the United States were more inclined to use hostile behavior when trying to influence others. Mothers in lower-class neighborhoods, for example, more often struck their children when disciplining them than did mothers from upper-class parts of town.

Middleton (1983) summarizes recent studies showing that the social class of board members affects their tendency to enter into disputes. She reports that board members from high socioeconomic levels avoid controversial topics and seldom allow their board to get into a conflict because their peers would disapprove of their displaying aggression. Middleton writes that boards with a majority of members from low socioeconomic levels more often get into disagreements, interfere with moves by their executive officer, and take it upon themselves to represent the managers (without the latters' knowledge) when conferring with parties outside the organization. She adds that these boards are more easily influenced by sources outside the board than boards made up of members from high socioeconomic levels. If a board contains several subgroups of low socioeconomic status, each with its own set of outside advisers, members often get into a dispute over whose advisers are correct.

Effects of a Conflict

When board members and nonmembers reach a standoff, the climate shifts within each group. Some of these changes are helpful for the groups, others are not. As a conflict develops, the leadership within each group tends to become centralized; members with the greatest influence, legitimate or not, take charge in meetings. The greater the threat from a rival group, the more members welcome this narrowing of authority and follow the most strongly assertive speaker (Mulder and Sterling, 1963). At the same time, the speed of discussion increases. Members talk more briefly, stick closer to the point, avoid tangents, press harder for agreements, and emphasize actions to be taken rather than a need for similarity in opinions. Group members play down differences among themselves in favor of finding common views. Members are more willing to go along with agreed-upon ideas instead of trying to have their own way (Zander, 1982).

Because their group is under outside pressure, members close ranks. They think well of their colleagues; express more confidence in one another than they did before the conflict began; and feel that they themselves, along with their suggestions, are valued by their colleagues. Any member who is to present the board's case in a meeting with a rival body is instructed by colleagues on what to say and is made to feel that a deviation from these instructions will be disapproved of. As a result, the representative enters negotiations with a stance that he or she does not have the right to change. This person is a communicator of the group's resolutions rather than a solver of a problem between the two groups.

A conflict tends to stimulate impatience and, in turn, aggression. Such hostile tendencies cause misperceptions, misunderstandings, and efforts to defeat rivals. Because of their anger, people who are usually levelheaded come to see malicious intent behind opponents' innocent actions. They distort comments made by rivals and make little effort to comprehend the others' statements. Worse, they exaggerate and mislead when making comments about members of the other group. During a conflict, members of both sides do not like ambiguity, so opponents oversimplify the issue and thereby further distort it (Zander, 1985; Zeigler, Kehoe, and Reisman, 1985).

In a dispute, members of each group see those people in the competing group as selfish and untrustworthy. Each side resists making a conciliatory move. This loss of trust is accompanied by a decrease in friendliness. People who freely associated before the disagreement begin to avoid each other. Members do not offer information to their rivals as they once did and may even provide incorrect information if it seems useful to do so. Participants in a dispute are less willing to try out new ideas and prefer to stick to old ways.

Useful Conflicts

Although conflicts can cause unfavorable consequences, some disputes are useful. Participants in a dispute may view contrasting opinions as stimulants to creativeness and jointly seek new and better ideas. An interchange between groups that disagree can awaken interest rather than defensiveness and rivalry. The conflict provides an opportunity to banish stagnant thinking and to generate useful uncertainty on both sides so that participants can recognize they have an issue to resolve (Pelz and Andrews, 1966). Thus, an intergroup dispute becomes a means for airing problems and giving them the attention they deserve.

Differences between groups can help each group change in favorable ways. A successful solution to a conflict increases the cohesiveness of a board and many useful group characteristics follow from an increase in the attractiveness of the group among members. Whether the course of an intergroup conflict becomes destructive or constructive depends in good part on how members go about resolving or controlling their conflict and on the similarity of objectives among conflicting parties.

Summary

A conflict exists when two parties disagree about what they should or should not do. A conflict is wasteful if the tension it generates prevents participants from thinking clearly or making sound decisions. It is useful if it awakens interest and curiosity, leading to creative efforts toward improving things and to the treatment of problems that have been unreasonably ignored.

A conflict is likely to arise if members of a board and a rival group want the same things and there is not enough for both, if members in each group block the achievement of the other group's goal, or if those on one side develop an emotional response to the style used by the others during discussion of their views.

A minor disagreement becomes a full conflict under certain conditions, including unclear roles for board members and nonmembers, lack of settled procedures for settling disagreements, members of one group feel they improperly receive fewer benefits than their peers, participants enjoy fighting, members of a board do not respect their CEO, colleagues on a board disagree with one another, or a crisis develops. A conflict may worsen if the two sides become polarized, emotions escalate, internal social pressures prevent participants from being broad-minded, the issue under discussion is important, the culture of the separate sides encourages hostility, or group members are from lower socioeconomic levels of society.

A conflict tends to centralize authority in a group and stimulate group members to close ranks.

8

Conflict Planning
Making Contingency Strategies for Settling Disputes

Members of a governing board seldom welcome a wasteful disagreement with others because hostile give-and-take is not usually board members' style. They prefer rational problem solving when a dispute arises. Yet conflicts do occur, even in a society of angels if the heavenly hosts differ over what *good* is (Banfield and Wilson, 1963). A conflict creates tension. Those involved want an end to the stress.

In this chapter, I describe procedures for resolving disputes that protect the dignity of the participants in a confrontation. These processes are intended to keep competing parties from suffering the expense and anger engendered by a lawsuit. They are useful when participants want to resolve their conflict in a way that benefits both parties to some degree. If either side refuses to change or rigidly insists on victory at the expense of rivals, no process can resolve a conflict, except binding arbitration or a lawsuit.

Preparing for Potential Conflict

Both individual board members and the board as a whole can prepare for a situation in which there may be a conflict. Through preparation, a conflict may be contained.

An individual board member can take several steps to avoid wasteful conflict. A board member knows that he and his colleagues are to meet in a decision-making conference with people whose opinions differ from the board's. In anticipating this session, he asks himself what will make this session satisfying for him and his associates. He will be most content, he resolves, if the separate views of participants are melded into a useful outcome for all, with a minimum of irrational argument. This is his major motive. As he plans for the session, he decides to behave in ways that can help such a result to occur.

The meeting is more likely to be useful, he determines, if the following happen during the session: He is proud of the ideas developed during the conference. He listens carefully to proposals offered by those on the other side, even though he cannot accept all of them. Some of his own notions are useful and participants indicate that this is the case. His style of participation (thoughtful, alert, fair) is imitated by others. He remains flexible in his outlook, does not stick to his own ideas no matter what. The other side fairly considers views offered by his board. He does not force the other party to yield by using coercive actions. And he resists the temptation to push the conference onto a sidetrack to prevent rivals from succeeding in their goals.

In working toward such potential sources of satisfaction, the board member prepares to do specific things before (and during) the meeting that might help make the meeting effective. He offers to join a few opponents beforehand to lay out ground rules concerning who will speak, for how long, and on what issues; what outcome is to be sought: who will sit where; and principles of decorum. He sharpens his thinking on the topic so that he can present his ideas clearly. He thinks through the advantages of his ideas, why his points are useful, and how he can defend them. He plans to listen attentively to others' ideas. He intends to evaluate their suggestions by using them, putting them in his own words, and seeing if they work. He will try to avoid behaviors that trigger resistance among listeners and, thus, he promises himself to steer away from

- Ridiculing those addressed: "There you go again." "You consistently do the wrong thing."
- Making arbitrary demands: "I want an answer now!" "Here is what I want you to do."
- Threatening to penalize listeners: "We will take you to court so

fast your head will swim." "Lots of us feel as I do, so I am going to organize a protest." "I warn you. I never back away from a fight." "So sue us."

- Using incorrect information: "All clinics make a profit. Why doesn't ours?"
- Employing hyperbole: "You are extortionists!"
- Urging a violation of the rules: "The bylaws are not clear on this action, so let's see if we can get away with it."
- Making ad hominem remarks: "You are stubborn." "You won't try to see both sides." "You are hopeless."
- Claiming innocence: "It's not my fault that you are soreheads. I try to make a simple point and you get mad!"

Board members as a group and the group of nonmembers can also plan how to dampen emotional behavior and enhance rational actions. Examples of the actions they can take are given here and are also available in writings by Deutsch (1973), Pruitt and Rubin (1986), Carver (1990), and Fisher, Ury, and Patton (1991) and in my previous work (Zander, 1982, 1990).

- Members of the board and members of the opposing group agree that they intend to work as problem solvers. Toward this end, they will suppress tendencies to be defensive, hostile, or fearful.
- Each group accepts that initial points of view might change during the joint discussion.
- Participants decide who is to make the final decision, if one is needed; who will have a say over what; and what rules will govern the choice of a decision.
- Participants agree to use the help of a third party, if necessary, such as a referee, mediator, or arbitrator.
- Participants decide what people on each side must do to earn and retain the trust of the other party. For example, they may agree to provide evidence for data they employ; bring in expert witnesses to support ideas that need such support; or refer to past similarities in the views, friendships, and motives among members on both sides.
- Participants settle on values that will guide them during the conference, such as fairness, accuracy, justice, equality, and rationality.

- Participants on both sides identify and stress the similarities between the objectives of board members and those of the opposition so that cooperativeness in the relationship can be enhanced.
- Because each side has similar goals, participants observe that acts by one party will move both sides toward these shared objectives. It is noted that goal-directed actions of any participant help all others as well.
- Participants declare that they will be more likely to find a useful solution if they consider many alternatives rather than a few.
- Participants demonstrate that they are prepared to talk openly and make concessions if necessary to attain a sound and mutually satisfying solution.
- Participants recognize, as do Fisher, Ury, and Patton (1991), that they may need to stop arguing in favor of the positions they prefer in order to identify the interests behind others' proposals and how these can be met.

Settling an Intergroup Conflict

If a conflict develops despite preplanning between a board and another group because participants ignore such plans, how can they resolve a dispute? Different degrees of disagreement demand different ways of resolving them. Therefore, this section discusses conflicts of several strengths, mild to severe, and several ways of dealing with each. Some of these procedures need no help from a third party because one of the participants can provide the limited leadership needed. Others require the assistance of an understanding person, and still others demand direction by a trained individual. The fairness or bias of a third party is not a real issue in any of these methods because in all of them (except for binding arbitration), a third party helps both sides reach their own resolution, one that is acceptable to both. He or she does not tell them what they must do.

Lively Discussion, But No Firm Disagreement

When an individual or a group asks members of a board to consider action on help they need, a problem that deserves the board's attention, or an opportunity that could help the board or its constituents, a lively discussion with no firm disagreement may result. The two parties are not in a sharp dispute, but each brings a different perspective to the issue at hand and finds it hard to understand the other's views. Members of the board are interested enough to examine the matter with those who raise it. For example, a group of parents may ask the school board to introduce a course on saving the environment, and the board may inquire about such courses at other school districts.

Fact Finding. If members of a board believe their major need is clarification of the central ideas (costs, concepts, contrasts) involved in a proposal brought by nonmembers, they may engage in a fact-finding discussion. Participants try to reach a common understanding of the situation under discussion, get the facts straight, or tell one another how they view the issues involved. The topics may be complex, emotionally involving, or new to people on both sides. Such discussion may be preliminary to a decision, but is not intended to settle the issue by itself.

Ordinarily, a fact-finding discussion is calming for all at the table. A relaxed response is fostered if participants come to the meeting with clear ideas about what they believe or know. Effective fact-finding requires that participants be precise in expressing their views and in understanding the ideas of others. The boundaries are open, and any topic is fair game. The only restrictions are those that both parties set ahead of time to ensure that an orderly process is followed.

Mild Disagreement

If a group brings specific problems, proposals for action, or both before a board, mild disagreement may develop over what should be done. Or disagreement can develop if the board discusses changes it might sponsor and word of this action reaches stakeholders who object. In a mild disagreement, members of the board believe that each side should have a say in reaching a solution and can use several procedures to get input from others.

Intergroup Problem Solving. If the number of possible solutions is limited, participants may employ intergroup problem solving, as described in Chapter Two. If a true crisis develops, however, the procedure that follows may be more effective because problem solving demands logical thinking, which, in the midst of a dispute, may be hard to maintain.

Method for Evaluating Potential Solutions. Sometimes the nature of a problem is clearly defined for all participants, and the characteristics of a good decision are well known, but too many noteworthy alternatives come up in a meeting. Choosing among these alternatives becomes the central issue, and a dispute arises over which potential solution seems most sensible. A procedure is needed to guide the process of selecting the best solution from those available.

A situation at the University of Michigan shows the problems that can develop when choices must be made between many alternatives. The regents of the university were asked to approve the construction of safer facilities for research in recombinant DNA, to be financed by federal funds. They appointed a committee of faculty members to advise them in this matter. A group of teachers and staff members designated themselves as critics of such facilities and of this kind of research. They made speeches, wrote stories for newspapers, and sponsored public forums, all intended to encourage disapproval of the research. They observed meetings of the officially appointed faculty committee, read articles and notes gathered by that body, and repeatedly presented their ideas to the regents.

The problem required a simple yes or no answer. But there were questions and suggestions concerning cost, safety, and the value of the work to be done. The regents were confused. They reached a solution, after many hearings, by listening to the pros and cons on each of eighteen crucial questions posed at a forum led by the president of the university. At that session, representatives of both sides sat across the table from the regents and spoke to these questions when asked to do so. After the questions had been answered, the regents were at last prepared to decide. They decided in favor of the research (Zander, 1979).

The choice of a solution from a number of alternatives can be facilitated by moving through a series of specified steps. Directing the problem solvers through this sequence is easy—someone must simply move things along. The procedure offered here is similar to one proposed by Levi and Benjamin (1976). It begins once the problem has been clearly defined and participants are sure they understand it.

First, all participants are asked to describe in writing the solution they prefer, one that they feel sure those in the opposing party do not want. These statements supply a variety of alternatives worthy of discussion because they are, by definition, controversial— one party wants what the other does not. The differences of opinion will stimulate interaction.

Second, each of the desired outcomes is written on a blackboard or a newsprint pad without identifying the author, and participants choose the one they wish to discuss first. They are to base their judgment on which one seems most important (relevant and likely to work) for the problem at hand. The majority decides.

Third, focusing on the outcome chosen above, people on each side give their reasons orally for favoring it or disliking it. These pro-and-con statements are listed on the blackboard.

Fourth, when a good number of pro-and-con statements have been given, each participant rates his or her degree of satisfaction with the solution under consideration. The rating scale runs from +10 to –10, with positive numbers indicating satisfaction and negative numbers indicating dissatisfaction.

Fifth, the participants select another potential outcome to consider as they did in the second step. They state their reasons for or against this potential solution and rate their satisfaction or dissatisfaction with it.

The five steps are repeated three or four times. This usually is enough because remaining options lose their appeal in light of the consideration given to those already discussed. A solution is then chosen using the information generated in this process.

This process separates the unitary step of choosing a solution into its components so that comments can be concentrated cleanly on each facet of making a choice. During this process, participants have in mind what has been said on each topic and why. As a result, chances are good that the participants will feel both sides have had adequate say on all relevant issues when making their choice.

Conflict Arouses Emotions

A conflict can arouse emotions that make the conflict more difficult to resolve. For example, advocates seeking change believe that board members plan to take action or have made moves that will reduce their satisfaction, effectiveness, or well-being. They urge the board to take a different direction, and this request is refused. During discussion of the issue, people on each side become irritated, competitive, or otherwise involved in winning rather than finding the wisest course of action. One situation, for example, that may arouse emotions is the announcement by a school board that children will be bused to schools away from their neighborhoods to foster integration of the schools.

The participants in this type of conflict agree that the state of affairs is intolerable and would like to resolve it. Two procedures that they can use to resolve the conflict are discussed here.

Method for Identifying Feelings. The substantive content of a dispute between a board and a set of critics may become a minor matter compared to the friction the conflict causes. Most board members learn to live with intergroup tension because they recognize that their position makes them convenient targets for constituents who wish to blame someone for their own misfortune. However, board members may decide it would be well to reduce the discomfort in relations with another group. They wish, in short, to identify and understand the origins of this stressful relationship.

Although the procedure to identify feelings is simple to pursue and does not demand a guide who is trained in human relations, it does require a discussion leader who is used to helping conferees work together on a complex topic. Both sides must agree to give the approach a try.

The following procedure is a modified version of one proposed by Bennis (1969). It begins with a joint meeting of the two groups, or subcommittees of them, in which group members are told what they will be doing. Each group then moves to a separate room, where participants discuss three questions in turn, for thirty to forty-five minutes each, and list their answers on separate sheets of newsprint. The three questions are (1) what qualities best describe our group? (2) what qualities best describe the other group? and (3) what qualities do we predict the other group will assign to us?

After each of these lists is completed, the separate groups reassemble and act thereafter as one. Taking up one question at a time, a spokesperson for each group explains the group's answers and responds to questions.

It is obvious at once that members of the two groups differ in their perceptions of themselves and members of the other group. Some of these views are wrong (on factual grounds), others are misperceptions or improper assumptions, and still others are surprisingly and painfully correct. Most of the remaining discussion turns to the origins of such contrasts and misunderstandings. The participants find themselves calmly considering delicate matters that they would have been unable to discuss previously without embarrassment, hesitation, and blaming. This exploration of insights usually satisfies participants; they feel informed and relieved. In some cases, they move on to the next logical issue, What can we do to improve the relations between our groups?

Intergroup Mediation. A board and a rival body are likely to request the help of a mediator if in a continuing dispute they tried to improve things but failed, are disturbed over the situation, or feel they cannot allow the conflict to continue. A mediator is a skilled leader of a problem-solving discussion. He or she helps the two sides reach an agreement about how relations between the two will change in the future. The participants, not the mediator, make these decisions, put them in writing, and promise to abide by them. Anything said in the session is confidential.

Mediators are not necessarily highly trained; some are ordinary citizens who have been taught how to do this job and work at it part time, for free. A mediator will not handle problems that need technical expertise, such as issues involving engineering, finances, or law.

The mediation procedure described here is based on work by Beer (1986). A mediator begins by explaining the process to be employed, offering encouragement to participants (who may be a bit uneasy), and describing a few ground rules. The mediation process involves four steps.

First, the mediator asks representatives from each side to tell their story: what happened, why, what they did, what others did or did not do, and so on. The representatives are allowed to speak without any interruption by listening opponents. Even though these accounts may be crafted to make the speakers appear in the best possible light, the listeners hear, usually for the first time, how members of the other group view things. The mediator takes notes and encourages full revelations but does not try to get the facts straight at the moment.

Second, the mediator asks participants to respond to questions, accusations, and issues raised by people on the other side. Facts, intractable differences in opinions or feelings, and shared views and agreements are identified. Displays of anger or other emotions are checked by the mediator.

Third, the mediator identifies major issues at the heart of the disagreement. He or she describes these issues, asks participants if they are the central matters, makes corrections where indicated, and leads participants into a discussion about what can be done about each issue. The ensuing plans are discussed in their smallest details while the mediator repeatedly asks if the ideas are practical, will work, and can be completed and who will do what and when. Often, both sides give up something to get important gains.

Fourth, the agreement is put into writing so its exact nature can be recalled in the future, if need be, and participants on both sides sign it. This paper changes the groups' relationship from that of being adversaries to being parties to an agreement, a most important transformation. Mediation moves participants from preoccupation with their problem to planning for the future, from distrust to willingness to take a chance.

Stalemate

Participants in a dispute may be unable to agree on a resolution to a specific conflict. They are at an impasse. Yet members of the board believe they cannot ignore the desires of those with whom they disagree. For example, the trustees of a private hospital refuse to give nurses an increase in wages, and the nurses, in retaliation, claim they are ill and cannot come to work. Residents of a condominium community protest when the developer proposes to direct the flow of a creek into an underground pipe. Regents of a university propose that no research be allowed on military weapons or other matters useful in war, but members of the faculty object. Participants in this type of conflict recognize that a suitable decision might be reached only by asking a neutral party such as an arbitrator or a judge to provide assistance. The suggestions that follow for resolving a stalemate are from Ury, Brett, and Goldberg (1988).

Advisory Arbitration. In advisory arbitration, a professional arbitrator is hired who hears evidence presented by both sides and gives a nonbinding opinion of the kind he or she would have rendered if this were a session where participants must obey the ruling. After the arbitrator's advisory opinion, the participants can see who would have won if this were binding arbitration. They may then plan their next steps: talk some more, try mediation, hire a binding arbitrator, go to court, enter into bargaining, and so on.

The costs are low in this approach because the hearings are brief and the advisory ruling is given orally and informally. Sometimes groups that got nowhere in intergroup mediation try this process to avoid the expense and formality of a regular arbitration hearing. Some courts demand the use of advisory arbitration in certain kinds of cases and will hear only those cases not resolved by such arbitration.

Minitrial. Another procedure that provides information opponents can use in deciding how to resolve their conflict is a minitrial. In this method, lawyers representing each side (or colleagues playing the part of lawyers) present evidence and arguments before people who are, or act as, judges. In some instances, these judges may be three respected members of the organization or community, accepted by both sides, who have no part in the conflict. After hearing the two parties, the three judges discuss the problem, evidence, and appropriate ruling in the presence of the rivals. They make their decision then and there.

This procedure, it should be noted, puts the argument into the hands of three people who are not emotionally involved, who hear both sides of the story, and who have the interests of both sides equally at heart. Their open discussion illustrates what a real judge might consider in making a finding, and it uncovers new insights that the contending parties may use if they wish to try again at settling the issue on their own.

Binding Arbitration. In binding arbitration, a neutral arbitrator listens to evidence presented by both sides and issues a ruling that all have agreed to obey. In the 1930s, about 10 percent of contracts for collective bargaining required binding arbitration of disputes between union and management. Today, 95 percent require such arbitration (St. Antoine, 1984). Boards elected by constituents (city councils or boards of religious congregations) often cannot enter into binding arbitration because they are forbidden by their charters to let anyone make a decision for them.

Zack (1984) says that an arbitrator, in contrast to a mediator, is more concerned with the substance of the conflict than with emotions aroused by it. At the outset, he or she asks participants to define the issue in terms both sides accept. Thereafter, the steps are not always the same and depend on the preferences of the arbitrator and of those taking part in the discussion. The arbitrator may set requirements such as a time limit, involvement of lawyers, degree of adherence to rules of evidence, and how much say both parties have in reaching a final decision. The arbitrator takes an active role, asking questions until he or she understands the issue, has the data needed to make a decision, and is confident that both sides agree on the pertinent facts. The relevance of the evidence is important, but legal rules of procedure are not always used. Some sessions are more like conversations than jurisdictional hearings.

In certain cases, it is easiest for an arbitrator to split the difference between opposing demands. If an arbitrator does this often, those groups who use this arbitrator on their next case may take inflexible, widely separated stands and refuse to compromise so that the difference cannot easily be divided by the arbitrator.

If the arbitrator is not able to make a fair ruling, he or she may ask the opposing groups to make their best, most conciliatory final offer. The arbitrator then chooses one or the other of these two as his or her decision. The potential consequences of a request for a final offer may be so threatening to participants that they withdraw from arbitration before a judgment is made and try to settle the matter on their own or by another means (Pruitt and Rubin, 1986).

Severe and Continuing Conflict

Opposing parties may become involved in a dispute, be unable to settle it, and remain opponents for a long time. Members of each group may be hostile toward the other and keep their distance, refusing to talk. This state of affairs may have carried on long enough to suggest that it will not fade away soon. But people in both parties come to recognize they must improve their relations for the good of the larger organization or their own. No specific problem is at the heart of the matter beyond the enmity between the two groups. For example, an association dedicated to preventing the growth of a community is opposed by one that favors increasing the town's size, or unionized workers who have been locked out for years by the board of a company are now wanted as employees because their skills are needed in a new program.

A procedure that will allow the two sides to find ways of communicating comfortably and usefully is desirable in such instances. The hostility between the two groups makes it unwise to bring the two together for a simple face-to-face discussion, as this has not worked in the past and would probably generate only angry interchanges now. The *interface conflict resolving model* of Blake and Mouton (1984) is appropriate in these cases. It requires group members or subsets who represent them to move through a sequence of steps. Each step takes a few hours, and the whole process may take three or four days. The steps are straightforward and the participants do all the work, so a director of this operation needs no special training. But the one in charge must be an experienced leader of discussions, with a background in human relations, such as a mediator or group counselor.

The leader begins the procedure by meeting with representatives of the two groups (six to ten people on a side), giving an overview of what is ahead, and sending each group into a separate room. First, members of the two sets are asked to describe the qualities of an ideal relationship between the two groups. These are listed on sheets of newsprint. The properties might concern attitudes that underlie intergroup relations, common goals, standards of excellence, ways of cooperating, and so on.

Second, the two groups assemble in one room. A spokesperson for each describes and explains items on its list. The two groups then work as a single entity to create a list of properties that would characterize an ideal relationship that both sides accept.

Third, the groups again meet in separate rooms and describe conditions that currently characterize the actual relationship between the two parties. If it is useful to do so, they identify past events that shaped this state of affairs.

Fourth, as in the second step, the groups work together again to create a joint description of the elements in the day-by-day relationship between the groups. Both sides must be able to accept this description as accurate.

Fifth, members of both parties, still meeting as one, now identify obvious gaps between the ideal and the actual relationships. They decide what changes are needed to close these gaps and plan how these transformations can be achieved.

Sixth, in about six months, the two parties meet to examine their success in resolving past hostilities. They also plan their next steps.

This approach has several beneficial characteristics. The participants' attempt to visualize an ideal situation at the outset gives them a task that is not embarrassing to discuss while freeing their imaginations. They begin to see how things could be improved. The gap between the ideal and the real relationships is a strong stimulant. Each group learns, in a noncontroversial setting, how others think about relations between the two groups and how the groups' views are similar and different. The director of this procedure has no say in the ideas created; he or she does not tell participants what to think or what their thoughts imply. The director mainly moves participants from one step to another and presses for decisions where necessary.

This procedure sets up a way of working among participants that enables them to deal with touchy subjects objectively; feelings are treated as facts. The procedure leads into topics that are usually avoided, such as contrasts in what values are most important, vested interests, status differences, prestige, rivalry, or why one side distrusts the other.

Summary

Each person who intends to take part in a meeting of two groups can plan how to help make the session effective and free of conflict. Members on both sides may, moreover, agree ahead of time on things they will do during the session to dampen emotional behavior and enhance rational effort.

Different degrees of intergroup conflict require different methods to resolve them. If the discussion is lively because of contrasting views, participants may engage in fact-finding or intergroup problem solving. If a mild disagreement develops, problem solving may be useful or a procedure to evaluate alternative solutions may be useful.

If a dispute arouses emotions on both sides, participants may examine the nature and source of these reactions or bring in a mediator who will help them do so. Should a stalemate develop, progress toward a resolution may be enhanced by requesting advisory arbitration, holding a minitrial, or having an arbitrator make a binding decision for the two parties. If a conflict is enduring and members of each party cannot meet face-to-face without becoming hostile, the interface conflict resolving model can help the two groups communicate about crucial aspects of their relationship without emotional interference.

9

Board Performance Review

Evaluating and Improving Board Effectiveness

The members of a governing board want their board to do well. If the board does well, they want it to do better. Raising their aspirations for the quality of their performance fits the accepted value in this country that a group should improve its score with each repetition of a task regardless of what that task is; practice makes perfect (Zander, 1971). Members are usually confident that their board is improving because they personally are learning more and functioning with increasing skill while they serve on the board, and they believe colleagues are doing the same.

Board members are used to evaluating their personal efforts or having them appraised by others in school, sports, work, or community activities. Yet in most boards I am familiar with, a board member seldom suggests that the board evaluate how well it is conducting its activities. Moreover, such a proposal is likely to meet with resistance (unless many things have gone wrong so that a critique is immediately required). Even though board members want their unit to improve, they are not eager to appraise each other's behavior or to express these appraisals publicly to identify what is wrong and what action might be taken.

This chapter considers the basic features of feedback and evaluation and gives a few examples of how board members can comfortably evaluate their board's work. It examines changes boards make to improve their effectiveness or efficiency. A board may de-

143

velop its own methods for appraising and improving its work in the light of suggestions offered here.

Throughout this work, I have mentioned actions that responsible members may make to help their board perform effectively. Some of these actions include strengthening members' desire for their board to do well, clarifying the mission of a board, helping members find good alternative solutions to a board's problems, using effective problem-solving procedures, encouraging members to take part in a discussion, sharing leadership of a board, choosing appropriate procedures for a meeting, developing useful standards for a board, resolving disagreements within a board, maintaining group harmony, making board actions acceptable to others, responding to external pressures on a board, improving a board's power to influence, and resolving a conflict with another group.

Basic Components of Feedback and Evaluation

To decide whether changes need to be made in their board's procedures, board leaders review past performance of the board and evaluate the quality of this performance. They do so by determining whether the board's actions meet the criteria of success members previously established for the board, that is, by determining whether the board is reaching goals members had chosen for its operations. As we noted in Chapter One, members of a board cannot evaluate how well the board is doing unless they have objectives for the board and are able to determine if those have been reached. The ends members select for their board are subject to change, as a result of evaluating the group's performance, just as a board's procedures are open to modification when necessary. A board that evaluates its performance and changes its objectives, methods, or both is engaged in a *feedback cycle* (Zander, 1971).

Lewin (1947) described the process of feedback within a group in an essay on social diagnosis and action. According to Lewin, a plan for group work exists when the purposes of the group have been defined, a relevant goal and the means for attaining the goal have been determined, and a strategy for action has been devised. He applies the basic principle of feedback (taken from mechanical engineering) to the social realm by assuming this plan should be flexible and subject to change as actions by the group make it necessary. Emphasizing the major proposition in such self-steering—that a means exists for determining the desired performance and the closeness of this performance to the desired state—Lewin then asserts that a discrepancy between the desired state and the actual performance leads automatically to a correction of actions or to a change in planning (Zander, 1971).

Typical stages in feedback cycle are shown in Figure 9.1. First, responsible board members choose the board's goal and the methods to be used in attaining it. Second, action is taken that affects the group, organization, and/or the environment of each. Third, information about the movement of the board toward its goal is obtained and reported to the board. Fourth, board members observe any deviation between the original goal and the board's performance. Fifth, desires members have for the board, their personal motives, and pressures from external agents influence members' reaction to this evaluation. Sixth, if the deviation between the board's level of attainment is larger than is tolerable to members, the members take steps to reduce this discrepancy, either by changing the board's actions in the future or by changing the group's goal.

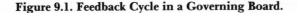

Figure 9.1. Feedback Cycle in a Governing Board.

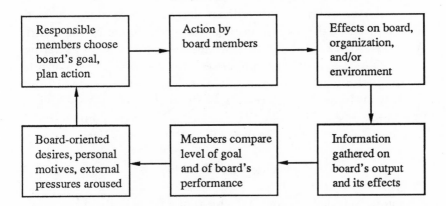

Source: Adapted from Zander, A., *Motives and Goals in Groups* (San Diego, Calif.: Academic Press, 1971), p. 5.

The feedback loop reveals the relationship between the board's performance and what is desired. When a feedback loop exists, members obtain evidence about the board's performance and will, if necessary, do something about the level of the goal, the board's way of working, or both.

Carver (1990) observes that members of boards for nonprofit organizations may prefer to evaluate the methods they use (that is, how smoothly their board functions) rather than their group's attainment of goals because the board's procedures for work are observable, but accomplishment of goals is hard to discern. Nonprofit boards wish to improve the world and it is difficult for them to determine if they have done so. To those people who believe it is harder to determine whether a board has attained its goal than to judge the value of the procedure used by the board, Carver (p. 80) says, "With respect to influencing organizational behavior, a crude measure of the right thing beats a precise measure of the wrong thing. . . . The best approach a board can take in program evaluation, then, is to stick rigorously to the result. . . . If it is worth doing, it is worth doing poorly if that is the best that can be done. But never, never forsake specifying the desired results in favor of a less crude evaluation." He also says that "only when the board has created ends policies should it stop to consider evaluation, because only when the board knows what it wants the organization to accomplish can it intelligently discuss evaluation" (pp. 79–80).

Carver's ideas about feedback and evaluation apply as well to appraisals of the staff of an organization overseen by the board. A board usually evaluates the staff, however, by simply evaluating the work of the chief executive officer since he or she is responsible for the performance of all subordinates. It follows that a board can sensibly evaluate the performance of the organization it supervises and propose useful changes in either its ends or means only if board members have set precise goals for the CEO (Carver, 1990).

Changing a Board's Purpose

Although its broad purpose is the heart of a board's life, the mission can lose its attractiveness if the conditions that originally stimulated the founding of the board (and organization) become less important to participants and the initial aim loses its usefulness. The participants in an organization may fully meet the desires they had when the organization was established, and the group's initial purpose may no longer appeal to them. Working toward the board's grand goals may have been gratifying to members at an earlier time but may no longer be gratifying, and members may lose their enthusiasm. Or they may see that their chance of reaching their original goal is poor and lose interest in that objective. Activities of a board may result in outcomes that are embarrassing to members so that continued effort toward the board's goal does not seem wise; the probability of repeated loss is too great.

A major reason that a board's mission may have little appeal to board members and is likely to be changed or neglected is that the board's mission is ambiguous and there is no means of measuring whether the board is meeting the objective. When members have a vague mission, they often are inclined to ignore it in favor of a clearer goal. For example, the board members of a church cannot accurately determine if they are helping members of the congregation achieve salvation, but they can reliably count whether the money in collection plates will be enough to pay off the mortgage. Board members prefer a precise objective because they want to feel that their board is moving toward its goal. They will not be satisfied unless the goal is attainable, they understand what they must do to achieve that end, and they are aware of their accomplishment when they achieve the goal. An unmeasurable or unattainable goal is not satisfying. A clear goal is more satisfying to board members even if it is not really an adequate substitute for the board's valuable but vague mission. Many boards doubtless ignore their higher mission in order to work toward more mundane and achievable objectives.

As noted earlier, a board with a fuzzy mission may turn to evaluating the methods it uses rather than the attainment of its goals. Board members may consider, for example, whether they have too few meetings, need more committees, should revise the treasurer's reports, want better publicity, or should hold more social functions. They do so, I believe, because these matters are easy to discuss and make decisions about. Members are not sure which procedure is best because they have no criteria of excellence. They make their decision on the basis of what is most convenient or easiest to perform. When such matters are the major interests of a board, it is easier for board members to determine if procedures have been performed accurately and what needs to be done to improve the unit's performance.

As noted in Chapter One, a board will seldom lower its goal because it typically prefers one that is a bit harder than its recent level of performance. Therefore, a board generally performs below the level of its goal more often than not and fails more than it succeeds (Zander, 1971, 1982).

External pressures influence board members as they consider whether to change their group's goals. Sources of these pressures are outsiders (clients, customers, patients) who depend on the services offered by the board's organization and try to influence its purposes; observers who compare the board's action with those provided by other boards; onlookers who comment on the board's performance; and individuals who have the right to issue orders about objectives for the board and the organization it oversees.

Some boards make a point of keeping the same mission indefinitely, regardless of performance, external pressure, or current relevance of the objective. For example, boards for religious bodies, liberal arts colleges, historical societies, fraternal organizations, service clubs, or insurance associations rarely change their mission. Such groups want stability and employ methods that protect them against change. The methods include established doctrines, revered beliefs, sworn pledges that members will abide by a board's charter, indoctrination of members in the organization's aims, and punishment of anyone who deviates from the group's prime purposes.

Evaluating Effectiveness and Efficiency

Along with determining whether their board has attained its objectives, members may want to know how much the achievement of the goal cost. Questions members consider when thinking about the cost of a goal include: How efficiently did the board operate? Was the gain worth the expense? What goal is this board failing to achieve? Why has this failure occurred? How should we change our procedures so that we can do better? How can we increase the efficiency of our board by reducing the amount of resources we expend in people, money, time, energy, or stress? What are the best characteristics of this board?

Board members can develop precise answers to such questions only if they determine, qualitatively or quantitatively, whether the board's objectives have been reached. If not, by how much did the board miss its objectives? The answers to these questions prepare board members to make more differentiated descriptions of a board's successes and failures.

Deniston, Rosenstock, and Getting (1968a, 1968b) offer methods members can use in making a detailed evaluation of a group's efforts. They suggest that evaluators limit their attention to one action at a time. An action, in their view, is an organized effort to eliminate a problem, engage in a program, or attain a particular end. An action has three features: one or more objectives; one or more efforts toward those objectives; and acquisition and use of resources such as money, personnel, time, or space. To evaluate a board's effectiveness or efficiency, each of these three variables must be measured. A precise description of a given action by a board, in light of these terms, is a statement that it employs specific resources to perform particular actions toward attainment of designated objectives.

Can a board's achievement of an objective be attributed to the steps taken under a given action? Deniston, Rosenstock, and Getting (1968a, 1968b) suggest that the effectiveness of an action can be analyzed through three numerical ratios. In one ratio, the score attained as the result of the action is divided by the score that would have occurred in the absence of that action. A United Fund, for example, may reach its financial goal in a campaign because it receives a large gift it did not ask for, not because its campaign solicitors sought and found enough givers, which was its planned action. Attainment of the goal in this case is not a measure of how well the solicitors acted in obtaining contributions.

A second ratio considers the total number of actions taken divided by the number that were supposed to have been performed. Board members who are busy but take none of the proper steps to reach their goal are not effective according to this ratio. A third ratio examines the total amount of resources expended divided by the amount of resources that were supposed to be used. A group that reaches its goal at more expense than intended is not effective.

The analysis by Deniston, Rosenstock, and Getting indicates that an action may be less effective than desired for several reasons. These include: assumptions about the links between objectives, actions, and resources were not valid; actions were not performed as intended; resources were not used as planned; or attainment of the goal was not measurable.

The efficiency of a given action is also of interest to a board because there is bound to be a limit to its resources. *Efficiency* is defined as the amount of resources expended by a board for a given level of goal attainment. Different aspects of efficiency can be computed with the use of several ratios suggested by Deniston, Rosenstock, and Getting (1968a, 1968b). In the first one, evaluators divide the number of objectives attained by the total amount of resources expended to determine the cost per objective attained. In a second ratio, the number of actions performed is divided by the resources expended to determine how much each action cost. And in a third ratio, the number of objectives attained is divided by the number of actions performed to determine the amount of gain provided per action. Clearly, board members who work through such ratios will develop a good understanding of their operations, where these succeed or fail, and at what cost.

Improving Meetings

Many board members prefer to deal with immediate and direct questions when evaluating how their board is doing. A useful set of such queries is proposed by Napier and Gershenfeld (1993), who suggest that responsible members ask themselves in meetings if they: "Create a positive atmosphere? Support and encourage participation? Listen and respond to varying opinions? Clarify statements or ask clarifying questions? Share opinions, feelings, ideas, and suggestions honestly and clearly? Help others stay on agenda topics? Identify and use resources within the group? Observe the group process and evaluate progress? Comment on interpersonal process issues when helpful? Encourage others in taking group-building and maintenance roles?" (pp. 451–452).

As in any group that holds meetings, members of a board may find it useful to take time to rate qualities that members wish to maintain or improve. This rating should be done privately and anonymously after the close of a session. A questionnaire used for this purpose is usually brief and uncomplicated. The ratings are summarized and are reported and discussed at the next session.

In one approach to a postmeeting evaluation, a respondent is instructed to rate aspects of the meeting on scales of one to five with endpoints like the following:

Very passive ———— Very active
Conflictful ———— Harmonious
Unsatisfying ———— Satisfying
Confusing ———— Clarifying
Dominated by a few members ———— Most members participated
Boring ———— Interesting
Leadership was not helpful ———— Leadership was skilled
We were rushed ———— Time available was adequate
Most agenda topics were trivial ———— Our time was well spent
We are inefficient in our discussions ———— We are efficient

A board that uses such a form discovers which aspects of its sessions are worth rating, what should be omitted from the form, or what other matters should also be examined. The averages of such ratings are not as important, of course, as the discussion among members on why a given quality is rated low or high and what needs to be done, if anything.

A wider array of characteristics than those listed on a form can be brought up for discussion by several informal methods. In one procedure, mentioned earlier (Chapter Three), observers sit at one side and watch the process events in the group, ignoring substantive ideas in the discussion. Comments by these observers are not judgments or evaluations; they are descriptions of interesting phenomena. When observers do their job well, the board members are eager to discuss their statements, either because they disagree with these statements, want to explain the occurrence of an event, or want to show how such an event could be prevented in the future.

In another procedure, groups of three to four board members

meet for about twenty minutes to think of questions they wish to address to officers of the board, chairpersons of board committees, or the chief executive officer. These queries may be in any depth, cover events that occurred in recent years, or look toward the future. The aim of the procedure is to appraise actions in the recent past (or ones coming up) and to consider what ought to be changed. A variation of this activity asks members of small groups to consider how the board (or the organization it guides) could be different if it were to start over. All small groups may consider the board or agency as a whole. Or each may be assigned a different topic, such as mission, facility, priority, financial support, clientele, organizational structure, or procedure.

Improving Communication

A frequent complaint within an organization or across boundaries of its separate departments is "lack of communication." One can never be sure what this statement means. It might signify that an individual feels ignored by others, forgot to talk to someone he or she is supposed to address, or is timid about speaking to another. Or it might indicate that the group members cannot get along or do not understand the meaning of certain statements. It is imperative that board members and the staff members of the organization the board governs keep in touch, say what they want to say, and get information they need. An unhindered flow of communication allows board members to collaborate in completing the board's regular activities and objectives. In an earlier work (Zander, 1982), I suggested methods that board members can use to improve communication with colleagues. Some of these methods follow:

- Making sure that members know one another's duties, talents, and problems so they can efficiently ask for and offer suitable information.
- Helping members be comfortable with one another by providing opportunities for them to associate freely at meetings and at special occasions.
- Demonstrating to a member that his or her ideas have been useful to colleagues.

- Making differences of opinion visible to members because if members are friendly, they will want to develop a common view and talk with one another to do so.
- Promoting cooperative relations among members and reducing rivalry among them.
- Reminding high-status members that their greater power makes them a threat to others. They need to take the initiative to make other members comfortable with them.
- Explaining to members that officers of the board are not rigid persons, have changed their minds in the past, and can be influenced by the rest of the board.
- Demonstrating to members that the fate of the board and the organization it supervises depends on open communication among board members and staff members.

Summary

Members of most boards expect the performance of their board to improve with practice, but few of them review and evaluate how well they have been doing so they can identify how their board might be changed. They need to appraise whether they are attaining their objective and if not, whether their goals, the procedures they use to move toward those goals, or both should be changed. A board that evaluates its performance and changes its objectives or methods, or both, on the basis of that evaluation is engaged in a feedback cycle.

If evaluators decide that the board's purpose should be changed because it is too hard, no longer useful, or lost its appeal, they need to avoid the temptation to set an objective that is too difficult. Instead, they ought to choose a level of achievement that is a challenge for the board, not too hard or too easy.

Board members should measure both the effectiveness and efficiency of their actions. Actions by a board may be less effective than desired because they were not performed as intended, resources were not used as planned, or the goal was so ambiguous that attainment of it could not be measured. Efficiency of an action is determined by measuring the amount of resources expended by the board for a given level of goal achievement.

The climate and quality of board meetings may be appraised by having members answer questions about meetings or complete brief postmeeting questionnaires. Discussion on different topics by separate subgroups of members is often useful. It is especially important that members evaluate the adequacy of communication among them and take steps to improve intermember give-and-take when necessary.

References

Bailey, F. *The Practical Uses of Passion*. Ithaca, N.Y.: Cornell University Press, 1983.

Bales, R. "How People Interact in Conferences." *Scientific America*, 1955, *192*, 31–35.

Banfield, E., and Wilson, J. *City Politics*. New York: Cambridge University Press, 1963.

Barker, R., and Gump, P. *Big School, Small School*. Stanford, Calif.: Stanford University Press, 1964.

Beer, J. *Peacemaking in Your Neighborhood: Reflections on an Experiment in Community Relations*. Philadelphia: New Society Publishers, 1986.

Bendiner, R. *The Politics of Schools: A Crisis in Self-Government*. New York: HarperCollins, 1969.

Bennis, W. *Organization Development: Its Nature, Origins, and Prospects*. Reading, Mass.: Addison-Wesley, 1969.

Blake, R. R., and Mouton, J. S. *Solving Costly Organizational Conflicts: Achieving Intergroup Trust, Cooperation, and Teamwork*. San Francisco: Jossey-Bass, 1984.

Bodenhausen, G., Gaelick, L., and Wyer, R. "Affective and Cognitive Factors in Intragroup and Intergroup Communication." In C. Hendrick (ed.), *Group Processes and Intergroup Relations*. Newbury Park, Calif.: Sage, 1978.

Brill, H. *Why Organizations Fail*. Berkeley: University of California Press, 1971.

Brown, C. *Putting the Corporate Board to Work*. New York: Macmillan, 1976.

Cabanatuan, M. "Jury Blames Richmond Woes on School Board." *Contra Costa Times*, June 1, 1991, p. 4A.

Camadena, M. "Brainstorming Groups—Ambiguity Tolerance,

Communication Apprehension, Task Attraction and Individual Productivity." *Small Group Behavior*, 1984, *15*, 251–264.

Cartwright, D. "Influence, Leadership and Control." In J. March (ed.), *Handbook of Organization*. Skokie, Ill.: Rand McNally, 1965.

Cartwright, D., and Zander, A. *Group Dynamics: Research and Theory*. New York: HarperCollins, 1968.

Carver, J. *Boards That Make a Difference: A New Design for Leadership in Nonprofit and Public Organizations*. San Francisco: Jossey-Bass, 1990.

Delbecq, A., Van de Ven, A., and Gustafson, D. *Group Technique for Program Planning*. Glenview, Ill.: Scott, Foresman, 1975.

Deniston, O., Rosenstock, I., and Getting, V. "Evaluation of Program Effectiveness." *Public Health Reports*, 1968, *83*(a) 323–335, (b) 603–910.

Deutsch, M. *The Resolution of Conflict*. New Haven, Conn.: Yale University Press, 1973.

Deutsch, M. "Fifty Years of Conflict." In L. Festinger (ed.), *Retrospections in Social Psychology*. New York: Oxford University Press, 1980.

Diehl, M., and Stroebe, W. "Productivity Loss in Brainstorming Groups: Toward the Solution of a Riddle." *Journal of Personality and Social Psychology*, 1987, *53*, 497–509.

Doyle, M., and Straus, D. *How to Make Meetings Work*. New York: Playboy Paperbacks, 1980.

Driskell, J., and Salas, E. "Group Decision Making Under Stress." *Journal of Applied Psychology*, 1991, *76*, 473–478.

Elgass, J. "Regents Vent Frustration with Open Meetings." *The University Record* (University of Michigan), Nov. 23, 1992, p. 4.

Ezekiel, D. "County Schools Board Is Thinking Smaller." *Contra Costa Times*, Dec. 29, 1991, p. 5A.

Fisher, R., Ury, W., and Patton, B. *Getting to Yes*. Boston: Houghton Mifflin, 1991.

Forsyth, D. *An Introduction to Group Dynamics*. Pacific Grove, Calif.: Brooks/Cole, 1983.

Forward, J. "Group Achievement Motivation and Individual Motives to Achieve Success and to Avoid Failure." *Journal of Personality*, 1969, *37*, 297–309.

French, J., and Raven, B. "The Bases of Social Power." In D. Cartwright (ed.), *Studies in Social Power*. Ann Arbor, Mich.: Institute for Social Research, 1959.

Funk, D. *Group Dynamics Law: Integrating Constitutive Contract Institutions*. New York: Philosophical Library, 1982.

Goldhammer, K. *The School Board*. New York: Center for Applied Research in Education, 1964.

Guzzo, R., and Waters, J. "The Expression of Affect and the Performance of Decision Making Groups." *Journal of Applied Psychology*, 1982, *67*, 67–74.

Hall, J., and Williams, M. "A Comparison of Decision-Making Performances in Established and Ad Hoc Groups." *Journal of Personality and Social Psychology*, 1966, *3*, 214–222.

Hollander, E. "Conformity, Status, and Idiosyncrasy Credit." *Psychological Review*, 1958, *65*, 117–127.

Holmes, G. *Student Protest and the Law*. Ann Arbor, Mich.: Institute for Continuing Legal Education, 1969.

Holsti, E. "Crisis, Stress, and Decision Making." *International Social Science Journal*, 1971, *23*, 53–67.

Janis, I. *Victims of Groupthink*. Boston: Houghton Mifflin, 1972.

Janis, I. *Crucial Decisions: Leadership in Policymaking and Crisis Management*. New York: Free Press, 1989.

Janis, I., and Mann, L. *Decision Making*. New York: Free Press, 1977.

Kipnis, D. *The Powerholders*. Chicago: University of Chicago Press, 1976.

Larson, C., and LaFasto, F. *Teamwork: What Must Go Right, What Can Go Wrong*. Newbury Park, Calif.: Sage, 1989.

Lebow, R., and Stein, J. "Beyond Deterrence." *Journal of Social Issues*, 1987, *43*, 5–71.

Levi, A., and Benjamin, A. "Jews and Arabs Rehearse Geneva: A Model of Conflict Resolution." *Human Relations*, 1976, *29*, 1035–1044.

Lewin, K. "Frontiers in Group Dynamics." *Human Relations*, 1947, *1*, 5–41.

Lippitt, R., Watson, J., and Westley, B. *The Dynamics of Planned Change*. San Diego: Harcourt Brace Jovanovich College Division, 1958.

Locke, E., and Latham, G. *A Theory of Goal Setting and Task Performance.* Englewood Cliffs, N.J.: Prentice-Hall, 1990.

Lorsch, J., and MacIver, E. *Pawns or Potentates: The Reality of America's Corporate Boards.* Cambridge, Mass.: Harvard University Press, 1989.

Mace, M. *Directors: Myth and Reality.* Boston: Harvard Business School, 1986.

Medow, H., and Zander, A. "Aspirations for Group Chosen by Central and Peripheral Members." *Journal of Personality and Social Psychology,* 1965, *1,* 224–228.

Middleton, M. *The Place and Power of Nonprofit Boards of Directors.* New Haven, Conn.: Institution for Policy Studies, Yale University, 1983.

Moore, C. *Group Techniques for Idea Building.* Newbury Park, Calif.: Sage, 1987.

Mulder, M., and Sterling, A. "Threat, Attraction to Group, and Need for Strong Leadership." *Human Relations,* 1963, *16,* 317–334.

Mullen, B., and Baumeister, R. "Group Effects of Self-Attention and Performance—Social Loafing, Social Facilitation and Social Impairment." In C. Hendrick (ed.), *Group Processes and Intergroup Relations.* Newbury Park, Calif.: Sage, 1987.

"Multiple Roles Compel Us to Look More Closely at What We Do." *University Record* (University of Michigan), Nov. 25, 1991, p. 12.

Napier, R., and Gershenfeld, M. *Groups, Theory and Experience.* Boston: Houghton Mifflin, 1993.

Nazario, S. "Crusader Vows to Put God Back into Schools Using Local Elections." *Wall Street Journal,* July 15, 1992, p. A1.

Nemiroff, P., and King, D. "Group Decision Making Performance as Influenced by Consensus and Self-Orientation." *Human Relations,* 1975, *28,* 1–21.

Newcomb, T. *The Acquaintance Process.* Troy, Mo.: Holt, Rinehart & Winston, 1961.

Osborn, F. *Applied Imagination.* New York: Scribner, 1937.

Park, D. *Strategic Planning and the Nonprofit Board.* Washington, D.C.: National Center for Nonprofit Boards, 1990.

Pelz, D., and Andrews, F. *Scientists in Organizations.* New York: Wiley, 1966.

Pruitt, D., and Rubin, J. *Social Conflict: Escalation, Stalemate, and Settlement.* New York: Random House, 1986.

Raven, B. "A Power Interaction Model of Interpersonal Influence: French and Raven Thirty Years Later." *Journal of Social Behavior and Personality,* 1992, 7, 217–244.

Reeves, C. *School Boards: Their Status, Functions and Activities.* Englewood Cliffs, N.J.: Prentice-Hall, 1954.

Rogers, E. *Diffusion of Innovations.* New York: Free Press, 1983.

Rohlen, T. "The Company Work Group." In E. Vogel (ed.), *Modern Japanese Organization and Decision-Making.* Tokyo: Tuttle, 1975.

Rothman, J., Erlich, J., and Teresa, J. *Promoting Innovation and Change in Organizations and Communities.* New York: Wiley, 1976.

St. Antoine, T. "Arbitration and the Law." In A. Zack (ed.), *Arbitration in Practice.* Ithaca, N.Y.: Cornell University Press, 1984.

Scott, W. *Values and Organizations.* Skokie, Ill.: Rand McNally, 1965.

Steinzor, B. "The Spatial Factor in Face-to-Face Discussion." *Journal of Abnormal and Social Psychology,* 1950, 45, 552–555.

Stone, C. *Where the Law Ends: The Social Control of Corporate Behavior.* New York: HarperCollins, 1975.

Thomas, E., and Zander, A. "The Relationship of Goal Structure to Motivation Under Extreme Conditions." *Journal of Individual Psychology,* 1959, 15, 121–127.

Thum, G., and Thum, M. *The Persuaders: Propaganda in War and Peace.* New York: Atheneum, 1972.

Tjosvold, D., and Field, R. "Effect of Concurrence, Controversy, and Consensus on Group Decision Making." *The Journal of Social Psychology,* 1985, 125, 355–363.

Ury, W. L., Brett, M. J., and Goldberg, S. B. *Getting Disputes Resolved: Designing Systems to Cut the Cost of Conflict.* San Francisco: Jossey-Bass, 1988.

Whyte, W. *The Organization Man.* New York: Doubleday, 1957.

Witteman, H. "Group Members' Satisfaction: A Conflict-Related Account." *Small Group Research,* 1991, 22, 24–58.

Wood, J., and Jackson, M. *Social Movements: Development, Participation, and Dynamics.* Belmont, Calif.: Wadsworth, 1982.

Zack, A. *Arbitration in Practice.* Ithaca, N.Y.: Cornell University Press, 1984.

Zajonc, R. "Social Facilitation." *Science,* 1965, *149,* 269–274.

Zander, A. *Motives and Goals in Groups.* San Diego, Calif.: Academic Press, 1971.

Zander, A. "The Purposes of National Associations." *Journal of Voluntary Action Research,* 1972, *1,* 20–29.

Zander, A. *Groups at Work: Unresolved Issues in the Study of Organizations.* San Francisco: Jossey-Bass, 1977.

Zander, A. "The Discussion of Recombinant DNA at The University of Michigan." In D. Jackson and S. Stich (eds.), *The Recombinant DNA Debate.* Englewood Cliffs, N.J.: Prentice-Hall, 1979.

Zander, A. *Making Groups Effective.* San Francisco: Jossey-Bass, 1982.

Zander, A. *The Purposes of Groups and Organizations.* San Francisco: Jossey-Bass, 1985.

Zander, A. *Effective Social Action by Community Groups.* San Francisco: Jossey-Bass, 1990.

Zander, A., Cohen, A., and Stotland, E. *Role Relations in the Mental Health Professions.* Ann Arbor, Mich.: Institute for Social Research, 1957.

Zander, A., Forward, J., and Albert, R. "Adaptation of Board Members to Repeated Success and Failure by Their Organizations." *Organizational Behavior and Human Performance,* 1969, *4,* 56–76.

Zander, A., and Gyr, J. "Changing Attitudes Toward a Merit-Rating System." *Personnel Psychology,* 1955, *8,* 429–448.

Zander, A., and Newcomb, T. "Group Levels of Aspiration in United Fund Campaigns." *Journal of Personality and Social Psychology,* 1967, *6,* 157–162.

Zeigler, H. *Interest Groups in American Society.* Englewood Cliffs, N.J.: Prentice-Hall, 1964.

Zeigler, H., Kehoe, E., and Reisman, J. *City Managers and School Superintendents: Response to Community Conflict.* New York: Praeger, 1985.

Index